GROW A VEGETABLE GARDEN IN POTS AND CONTAINERS

A REGIONAL GUIDE TO SMALL SPACE VEGETABLE AND HERB GARDENING IN AND AROUND THE HOME

Percy Sargeant

HIGHEST HILL Publishing

© **Copyright - Highest Hill Publishing - 2022 - All rights reserved.**

The content contained within this book may not be reproduced, duplicated, or transmitted without direct written permission from the author or the publisher.

Under no circumstances will any blame or legal responsibility be held against the publisher, or author, for any damages, reparation, or monetary loss due to the information contained within this book. Either directly or indirectly. You are responsible for your own choices, actions, and results.

Legal Notice:

This book is copyright protected. This book is only for personal use. You cannot amend, distribute, sell, use, quote, or paraphrase any part, or the content within this book, without the consent of the author or publisher.

Disclaimer Notice:

Please note the information contained within this document is for educational and entertainment purposes only. All effort has been executed to present accurate, up-to-date, and reliable, complete information. No warranties of any kind are declared or implied. Readers acknowledge that the author is not engaging in the rendering of legal, financial, medical, or professional advice. The content within this book has been derived from various sources. Please consult a licensed professional before attempting any techniques outlined in this book.

By reading this document, the reader agrees that under no circumstances is the author responsible for any losses, direct or indirect, which are incurred as a result of the use of the information contained within this document, including, but not limited to, — errors, omissions, or inaccuracies.

Contents

Epigraph	VII
Dedication	VIII
Introduction	1
1. Starting Your Garden	11
2. Creative Garden Structures	33
3. Vegetable Choices and Regional Gardens	49
4. Soil Science Basics and Composting Magic	65
5. Vegetable Planting and Growth. Seeds and Seedlings	85
6. Dealing with Plant Pests	108
7. Understanding Growing Seasons in Different Regions of the World	115
8. Harvesting and Preserving Vegetables	131
9. The Wonders of a Greenhouse	143
10. Handling Herbs at Home	155
Conclusion	165
Percy Sargeant Writer and Filmmaker	167

Acknowledgments 171

All nature is but unknown to thee;
All chance, direction which thou canst not see;
All discord, harmony not understood;
All partial evil, universal good;
And, spite of pride, in erring reason's spite,
One truth is clear. 'Whatever IS, is RIGHT'

~ Alexander Pope 1688-1744

For my dear mother and father.
In life, we loved you dearly, in death we love you still.

Introduction

Want to experience the sheer joy of choosing fresh and organic produce from your backyard? Sick of paying extra money for subpar and so-called fancy "organic" veggies displayed at your grocery stores? Well, you've come to the right place. Whether you are a newbie or someone with experience growing vegetables and herbs, this book will surely leave you with a few more tips and tricks up your sleeve.

I remember getting into the art of gardening myself for the very first time. I had just watched one of those gimmicky videos on YouTube where you drop the end of your leftover lettuce in a pot of water, and voila! You have some lettuce growing in a glass of water. Well, it is safe to say things didn't quite go as planned. Not only did the root of the lettuce not grow out beautiful branches, but it turned into one soggy mess.

Long story short, after a couple of hit-and-miss projects, I finally developed into a rather crafty and handy gardener. Not to sound too full of me, but my backyard is a gardener's dream come true. My garden is full of life, from herbs like parsley and basil to vegetables, including tomatoes and vibrant green peppers. Weekly pasta nights also become a must, especially when you have fresh produce at hand. Not to mention the fresh herbs that jazz everything up and turn your dinner fancy without you even trying! And trust me when I say this: the food you grow by yourself always tastes better.

Always.

The point of narrating my experience wasn't to show off my skills, although I don't really mind, but to let you know that I relate to your problems. Trust me when I say I have been in your short wellies as a first-time gardener. I understand how your heart might sink at the thought of being an irresponsible parent to your baby plant. The dreadful smell of wilting and withering might just be acting as the cherry on top, but you just can't resist the feeling you get when you grow your own produce, can you?

Well, you don't have to!

I have had my fair share of gardening mishaps that, I'm sure, we all can relate to. I've also succumbed to the growing trend and am trying somehow to harvest acai berries in my tiny backyard garden. Embarrassing, I know. Most of us think about gardening as just planting some seeds randomly and watering them whenever we feel it's looking a little "dry" while expecting them to grow into a great plant. As if.

GROW A VEGETABLE GARDEN IN POTS AND CONTAINERS

I realize that most of us just want the satisfaction of witnessing the healthy growth of our plants and then later harvesting those gorgeous and vibrant veggies. Somewhere inside of us horticulturists, we all want to bake a beautiful ratatouille with fresh and organic vegetables that we pick out from our backyard and be smug about it on our Instagram stories. Most of us have made unsuccessful attempts and want to better ourselves by learning to grow and parent our plants correctly.

This book is here to help you grow your little backyard garden. Some of you might not even be interested in a full-fledged backyard garden and leaning toward indoor plants. Not to worry! That is a comparatively more straightforward job since it doesn't require the raised bed containers essential for outside plants. That crucial construction is more of a challenge. But no need for any apprehension because you will be provided with all the details regarding the raised bed containers for ultimate success in your gardening endeavors.

Along with providing tips and tricks regarding your first-time gardening experience, I shall also educate you about the background and environmental features and aspects of growing your plants. For example, how important are climatic conditions when it comes to gardening and the growth of a seed?

Well, it's safe to say that it is everything! Plus, you must take into consideration the reality of global warming and its consequences on gardening. Rising temperatures can monumentally affect the growth of your plants. The changing seasons will inevitably influence how your plant grows. As temperatures rise and seasons change, aspects like humidity and light will differ at every change. From the frequency of the precipitation to the length of seasons, every one of these factors has both direct and indirect effects on plants and their growth. The impending frost will cause people to start planting much earlier. It just goes to show that there is a plethora of factors that you need to consider and take into account before planting a certain seed.

You might be wondering how I am the right person to take all this gardening advice from, especially considering I have messed up on more than one occasion.

Well, as far as my qualifications regarding this subject are concerned, I have studied zoology and botany, which, in their essence, deal with the biology of plants.

Furthermore, I have always been close to nature due to the environment of my home. My family and I have always encouraged a mini zoo in our house, from dogs and cats to tortoises and exotic birds. Along with that, my father was an avid gardener with his own greenhouse present in the middle of our home. With the help of this, he cultivated some of the most exquisite orchids I have ever seen in my life.

GROW A VEGETABLE GARDEN IN POTS AND CONTAINERS

With experience as a cinematographer during my career, I have made many films centered around nature. I have always wanted to share the plants and animals that coexist with us on this earth. From the life cycle of the mayfly on the Mississippi River; to the hand pollination of the extraordinarily endangered, wild Brighamia Insignis plant (cabbage on a stick) growing on the rugged Na Pali Cliffs in Hawaii, I want to showcase both sides of the coin.

All in all, through my parents as well as my field of study, I have great respect for nature. And it is hard to express in words how rewarding it is to plant your own seeds and then witness them growing. It is somewhat akin to watching your children grow up, hence the term "plant parent."

I genuinely feel that cultivating life is the essence of who I am. This book is also a kind of tribute to all that I have created regarding plants. But before I get into the details of different methods to grow your vegetables and help you choose the right one, you need to remember that not every plant thrives in a garden. So, make sure you walk down that road and select only the seeds suitable for your special garden. Also, be aware that there can be a certain amount of pleasure in looking out for pests and preventing all those nutritious veggies from getting destroyed. This way, you can avoid the dreaded mess and the disappointment.

PERCY SARGEANT

Allow me to let you in on a little fact from history: basically, the ancient Mesopotamian civilization that settled in the Fertile Crescent chose to start farming. And due to the fertility of the land, they were successful in producing a good number of crops and food. Thus, they did not feel the need to migrate from an area with a prominent food source. This shows how satisfying it is to actually grow your own food and how self-sufficient you get from this.

From what I feel, this book may even turn those who view gardening as a boring hobby into gardeners and plant lovers. Witnessing the art and miracle of a growing seed will surely take their breath away.

When it comes to seeds, they don't serve any purpose for years, existing in a dormant state, but once they are nurtured with the right climatic conditions, water, sunlight, and care, they thrive and grow into stunning plants. Hence, proving that these little blobs hold the power to provide you with nutritious vegetables, beautiful flowers, sturdy trees, and delicious juicy fruits! How delightful it is to buy seeds from a market and plant them in tiny jars and watch them transform.

Every seed has a lifespan of its own. For example, it's difficult for peppers and corn to grow once the seed crosses the two-year mark. However, carrots and tomatoes can last for up to four years. Oh, and lettuce and cucumbers beat them all, surviving for six years! All you need to do is store the seeds in the vegetable drawer, so they don't lose their magical powers too soon.

Through this book, that is, enriched with my experiences, I have more than a few techniques and pointers up my sleeve that will help each and every one of you overcome any disasters and problems. First and foremost, it is critical to plant a seed when the time is right. You must always take into consideration the weather characteristics and whether you can provide the optimum temperature for the seed to grow. For example, we know that peppers, tomatoes, and cucumbers are summer plants; hence, they need a warmer climate to grow. On the other hand, broccoli and peas are considered to be winter plants and thus need a cooler environment. So, make sure the perfect amount of sunlight is available because photosynthesis cannot occur without it. Wouldn't it be much easier if you could feed a plant your leftover espresso shot? Since you cannot, adhering to the plant's requirements is critical, to say the least.

In addition to this, it is crucial to have some shade around, too, since you don't want to leave your seedlings out to burn! I will touch on the exact conditions for different plants later on in the book since I don't want to give out all my secrets just now!

Another basic tip is to avoid crowding the plants and planting all the seeds at once. Instead, go for stagger planting, where you plant the first batch, and then after a few weeks, you plant the next one to harvest at different times. Focus on regional planting as much as possible. Several regional calculators are present online to guide you with the dates and time periods!

You really need to be down for the experience of the first year of gardening with an open mind. You need to have the determination and care to nurture your plant like it is your baby. You should have all the details at your fingertips; the sunlight, water requirements, length, etc. You should note every change and every little red flag, just like the ones you ignored in your ex. It is vital that you don't ignore them here. When it is the growing season, have a pen and diary in hand and write down every detail you notice regarding their growth. Please don't avoid doing this. I know it seems like a lot but trust me when I say this, it will all be worth it in the end.

The key to being a good gardener is patience. Patience is one of the most crucial qualities this book will instill in you. I won't be just listing down a monotonous to-do list. It is more than this. It is about submerging yourself in the art of planting and falling in love with it. Not going to lie; there will also be some reality checks, like the fact that it's not always rainbows and unicorns in gardening. There are some challenges you might face, like pests and insects. Not so hunky-dory, but rather annoying and disgusting, right?

GROW A VEGETABLE GARDEN IN POTS AND CONTAINERS

One of the best ways to spot disease is right in the beginning when the color of the leaves of your plant starts to change. That is discoloration. Check if they have holes or if the plant seems stunned. You must nip the evil in the bud instantly.

All in all, I just want to spread my love of plants through this book. The joy of being a plant parent. The satisfaction of walking into your backyard and choosing to cook dinner based on your variety of veggies. Not the cooking part, though; that's on you.

So, gear up because we are not here to lose. We are here to give those fancy organic grocery stores a run for their money. We are here to be self-sufficient and reliant. Keep reading for all the secrets to growing your own sustainable garden full of vibrant produce to give you all the nutrition that you deserve!

Chapter One

Starting Your Garden

They say too many chefs spoil the broth. The same goes for small-space gardening; planting too much in too little will turn out to be disastrous, especially when you are just starting out. My primary goal in this first chapter is to target the start of your garden, and we must consider the kind of space available. I want to cover everything from the space required for certain vegetables to how to build your garden from scratch. So, consider it Gardening 101.

One of the essential factors is planting in the ideal location. You need to make sure to choose a perfect spot to grow your new vegetables. For example, generally speaking, most vegetables require a site that receives direct sunlight for approximately 6 to 8 hours daily.

There are only a few types of vegetable plants that can endure shade. These are mostly the leafy ones. Some people struggle with soil with an inferior drainage system that allows water to stay stagnant.

If this situation pertains to you, the best plan is to plant your veggies in a raised row or even raised beds if possible. Doing this will significantly allow your drainage to get better. Plus, those with rocky soil might want to remove those rocks and tidbits since these hinder the growth of your plant's roots, resulting in weak plants.

Another vital point to consider while planting your veggies is to choose a place not subjected to strong winds. Winds too strong might topple over your small plants while increasing the risk of breakage. Plus, pollinators might also suffer and be unable to do their jobs. Plus, you don't want to pick a place that suffers from flooding or too much foot traffic.

The soil also matters. Your soil is the food for your plants; it's as simple as that. Besides being rock-free and drain-worthy, your soil should also be nutrient-rich. Lesser nutrients in soil would ultimately mean less food for the plant to grow healthy. Thus, the key is to provide your soil with all the organic nutrients for healthy plants. All in all, just don't plant in a spot that might enrage the Red Queen to say, "Off with your head!".

What to Do and Where to Do It

Sizing it all up.

The next step is to choose the size of your garden. Now we may be tempted to go all out and plant all kinds of vegetables in a large space. Sure, you could do that if you want to have your pantry flooded with peppers or tomatoes. Keep this in mind: it is better to have a small garden that makes you proud rather than a large one that frustrates you.

The key is to not plant too much too soon. So, start small. Grow the things you know you like to eat, that's including the rest of the people in your house. The size of your garden is crucial when starting out. The manageable area of your gardening space would range around 10 by 10 feet (3.05 x 3.05 meters), that is, a 100 square feet area (9.29 square meters).

GROW A VEGETABLE GARDEN IN POTS AND CONTAINERS

After choosing the size of your space, you can easily pick 4 to 5 vegetables of your preference. For some of you who require planting vegetables in raised beds (I will be elaborating on them shortly), a good and manageable size for beginners is around 4 x 4 feet (1.22 x 1.22 meters) or 4 x 8 feet (1.22 x 2.44 meters), depending on your preference.

However, if any of you still want to invest in a bigger garden, the largest you can work with easily is 12 x 12 feet (3.66 x 3.66 meters), considering you are just starting. Any bigger than that would be too hard to manage and might spoil all the fun and joy of having a veggie garden.

Let me give you a better idea of what it is to have a manageable-sized garden. For example: "Three hills of yellow squash, one pile of zucchini, ten different peppers, six tomato plants, twelve okra plants, a 12-foot (3.66 meters) row of bush beans, two caged cucumbers, two eggplants, six basil plants, one rosemary plant, and a few low-growing herbs like oregano, thyme, and marjoram might all be found in a garden that can sustain a family of four" (The Basics of Planting and Growing a Vegetable Garden, 2021).

However, regardless of the size of your garden, you just need to ensure that there is enough space for you to walk to harvest or weed around it. For this, you might need to create a walking space every four feet (1.22 meters) so you can reach the center of the space. Basically, just avoid stepping on the soil directly; otherwise, you might damage your soil and ruin the garden.

Choosing the Veggies to Grow?

The most exciting part of gardening is choosing your vegetables. Choosing easy, convenient, and productive vegetables is the key to starting out as a gardener and being successful. It is better to contact the expertise of horticulturists in your area and ask them about the vegetables that grow best in the area. For example, if you live somewhere that experiences cooler temperatures, vegetables that prefer warmer conditions might struggle to grow.

Some of the most available and most convenient vegetables to grow are as follows:

- "Lettuce
- Green Bean
- Radish
- Tomato (a bushel variety or cherry are easiest)
- Zucchini

GROW A VEGETABLE GARDEN IN POTS AND CONTAINERS

- Pepper

- Beet

- Carrot

- Chard, Spinach, or Kale

- Pea" (The Basics of Planting and Growing a Vegetable Garden, 2021).

You can also mix in flowers in your plant garden. For example, marigolds make the most amiable flowers. They keep away harmful pillagers while simultaneously attracting pollinators, and, well, who doesn't like some vibrant color in their garden?

Now let us discuss some rules while considering what vegetables to plant. Here are some tips to make the task easier for you all. Firstly, consider what you or your family members like to consume. Don't plant some eggplants just because you would enjoy the color or because it is easy. If none of you like to eat it, there is no point in putting in so much effort just to see all those beautiful purple eggplants rotting on the counter in some fancy basket. Don't bother planting something that nobody likes to eat.

The second point is to be mindful and realistic when planting vegetables. If, for example, you have several kids in your family, you might want to consider the amount and the kinds of veggies you consume daily. If you are not a veggies fan, don't plant too many since they would just go to waste. Of course, you could give them away to your friends, but what is the point of working yourself to the bone and taking care of your plants when you won't even be consuming them? Food for thought. Literally.

Another good tip is to consider what is already available in your area. Suppose your grocery store is filled to the brim with cauliflower and zucchini. In that case, you might want to plant something that is not readily available.

What is the point of growing a plant that is available everywhere around you? Plant something that will genuinely excite you to eat it! For example, some vegetables just taste a lot better when homegrown. These include tomatoes as well as lettuce or other leafy greens.

Another point to be noted is that herbs available in your local grocery stores are usually in dry form, and the ones available fresh are expensive as hell. So, grow your own herbs. They are convenient and can elevate any dish of yours!

When choosing your veggies take into consideration their optimum growing season. For instance, if you have planted tomatoes, you might want to say goodbye to your vacation plans. Since they grow the most in the mid-summer season, you need to be there to take care of them. If not you, then you might want to hire someone who can do this job for you while you are away. Neglecting them during the season; they thrive the most is certainly not recommended because you won't be able to witness the fruit of your efforts.

Last but definitely not least, please, for the love of God, choose good quality seeds. Even if they cost an extra dollar, do not skip this part. Otherwise, all your hard work and labor might be in vain.

Now I know that seed packets are cheaper, but the fact is that if the seed doesn't germinate, all that water and nutrients will go to waste—all of it. Not opting to spend a few extra cents will only result in you regretting your decisions in the long run. Growing a few plants of the same kind is easy. But, if you are going for the full ride and want to plant an assortment of veggies in your garden, you might want to educate yourself a bit more.

When and Where to Grow and Thrive

Better yet, where would these plants go?

If you are struggling with these questions, then look no further. I am here to assist you with my expertise. Let me give you a few basic guidelines to help you plant your plants perfectly. Do not expect to plant all the seeds you brought for your favorite veggies at the same time. As mentioned before, every vegetable has a growing season depending on the optimal climate conditions. For example, broccoli is a vegetable that likes cooler weather and should be planted in early spring or late winter. Similarly, tomatoes and cucumbers are summer vegetables and, thus, should be planted as soon as the soil begins to warm up a little.

Another tip is that if you plan to grow tall plants such as that corn, you might be better off planting them on the northern side of your garden. These long plants won't shade the rest of your garden. If you still get shade or there is already a shady part of the garden, you might want to plant shade-loving vegetables there. These vegetables are cool-seasoned and shade loving, similar to broccoli and other cruciferous ones.

Now, most vegetables are usually cyclically planted yearly; the plantation process is repeated. But if you are choosing to grow "recurrent" vegetables, that is, they do not require planting every year, you might want to consider permanent spaces for them. You could get raised beds for these kinds of veggies, including asparagus and other herbs.

It is important, as plant parents, to accept that each crop differs from the rest. Some, like tomatoes, have extended harvesting and maturity periods. In contrast, others have extremely short maturing and harvesting periods, like radishes. When you buy your seeds, the seed packet may indicate this information, or your seller or gardener might tell you these details themselves.

Stagger Your Seed Planting

Another crucial element to planting is "staggered seeds." Don't just plant all your seeds at once. I mean, what are you going to do with 25 lettuce heads ready to harvest at once? Sure, by all means, you could give them away to the poor and needy. Charity is always something to admire. Thus, you must stagger and plant seeds a few weeks apart. That way, you will have your veggies ready to use whenever you have finished the others. Just go to your garden and pluck whichever head is ready, and you are all sorted.

Raising Plants in Raised Beds

If you remember correctly, I mentioned the raised garden beds idea for perennial vegetables or soils with poor drainage. As promised, I will elaborate on these interesting garden inventions. In other words, raised beds are merely soil banks developed at a height and are often framed by either a wooden or another material fence. The soil is usually mixed with compost for nutrition. These prove to have an excellent drainage system. Raised beds are also a great option for people who suffer from having rocky, contaminated soil or just overall nutrient-less soil. Apart from putting them on soil or the ground, they can even be placed on other surfaces like hard floors. If you have shade-loving plants, a shade made up of cloth may very well be attached with a couple of hooks and hoops.

PERCY SARGEANT

Since I have already provided you with a brief outlook on what raised beds are, I'm going to discuss the size of raised beds and what size is suitable. Considering that most of us are home gardeners and not commercial ones, a narrow raised bed that is not more than 4 feet (1.2 meters) wide would be the best choice. This way, you can easily reach the center of the plants without overstepping on any of the soil. By creating bigger ones, you risk stepping on the soil and compacting it while destroying the structure around it. These raised beds are the best option for folks with limited mobility since they do not require an extreme bending-over posture. Thus, making them accessible for even those in wheelchairs, especially if built upon raised surfaces.

We have talked about how raised beds are a great pro technique that can be used even by beginners and how they add diversity to your garden. Raised beds can make the most out of all the outdoor space available to you because you can also place them on hard surfaces and platforms. That includes your patio, terrace, balcony, driveway, rooftop, backyard, or even your indoors! One of the pros of keeping raised garden beds is that they clear any lanes of weeds and are also great for dodging any pests, including, but definitely not limited to, snails and slugs in your garden. Furthermore, apart from vegetables, you can grow almost any plant you like in these beds. So, go ahead and plant away, whether it's basil or some vibrant perennial flowers.

You can find a variety of premade raised beds at your local nursery or even at Amazon or other gardening-related sites. There are options for tall raised beds that don't require you to bend down to take care of them. Some beds are tiered, while some come fenced already. The options are countless. Some even come with different compartments where you can grow an assortment of veggies, herbs, or even flowers to add some color to your monotonous garden.

Some people want to experience the joys of gardening but don't have enough space. Well, not to worry, I've got you guys covered! There are different ways to grow your garden.

Contain Your Gardens. Literally

For those of you who lack the space, start container gardening! Whether you have a gardening space that is too small or only have a patio, balcony, or even a driveway, you can start this hobby.

So, what is container gardening? Well, it's pretty simple; gardening in containers! Don't have the space? No problem. Start growing in pots instead of raised beds, and well, you'll reap what you sow.

Now let me start with a step-by-step guide for those of you who are beginning with container gardening. The key is to place your pots in a spot that gets a minimum of 3 to 5 hours of direct sunlight daily. Obviously, leafy greens can survive on less sunlight. Still, if you want those juicy cherry tomatoes, you need that sunlight. Believe me; your veggies need it.

Apart from keeping them in direct sunlight, make sure to put them somewhere that you can actually reach with your water pipe. What's the point of placing your plants in a spot if you can't even water the poor fellas? Plus, container garden plants require more water than regular ones. During the season, keep them in a safe place where they are not exposed to strong winds since that could strip them of moisture and even topple them over.

The size of your containers also matters a lot. If you don't pick the right one, all that effort could go to waste. A rule of thumb is that the more space for the roots, the better. A 5-gallon pot is perfect for a vegetable like a tomato since most veggies require a 12-inch (30-cm) root growth space. A smaller pot could work for any leafy greens like lettuce or spinach since they don't have long roots. You need to make sure that your pots have drainage holes. Standing water will lead to the growth of fungus or bacteria that might kill your plant. A standard drainage hole should be ¼ inch (0.6cm) in size and no more.

As far as the material of the pots is concerned, there are three basic options: fabric, ceramic, or plastic. But apart from this, you could literally use anything as a container for your plants, hanging baskets, or old wooden barrels; get creative!

Similar to raised beds, you might want to use soil known as "soilless" that comes in a mix for your containers. Avoid using soil from your garden. These soils are too heavy and risk getting waterlogged. And we definitely don't want that, now, do we? These soilless mixes contain nutrients like coconut coir and other things like limestone and fertilizers for the soil's strength.

Water. More or Less

Now a lot of people are concerned and a little apprehensive about watering pots, so let me tell you some tricks and tips about watering these bad boys. Firstly, you don't need a hose just to water these containers or pots. You can just about use anything! An old-school watering can also is a great idea.

Now, the first and most important thing to do is to water your plants in the morning. Doing this ensures the plants have enough hydration to last them through the day, especially through midday when they experience sunlight and warmth. Consider it a rule of thumb to water as early as possible.

Similarly, watering early in the day will make sure that the plant's leaves dry by the time night falls. This way, there will be no wetness on the leaves and no risk of some bacteria or fungus.

Many people just spray the water sparsely upon the upper structure of the plant and call it a day. No, the key is to water deeply because the roots of the plant require the most water and moisture in order to grow. The best evidence that you have watered correctly is that the water will run out of the bottom of the pot, and the soil will display a lot of saturation.

The second mistake that people make is watering the plant in smaller doses every few hours. This is the worst mistake that you can make as a plant parent. It is better to water deeply just once than to be stingy with it and do it after short durations. Please refrain from doing that. It creates shallower and weaker roots, and your plant will eventually struggle to hold up.

Container gardening is one of the best types of gardening and has many benefits. The best part is the ability to move the pots and containers whenever you feel like they are growing. You cannot do this in a garden where your plants are embedded in the soil.

Another great advantage is that you get to utilize a lot of space. You can put container plants anywhere from patios to your driveways and even your balconies. Container gardening also allows you to have a lot of control over your plants. You get to oversee the growth and choose your medium and nutrients. The great thing about this is that there are hardly any weeds, which makes the process much cleaner and more convenient. Harvesting is also considerably cleaner!

Plants Like to Grow Up

Another great option for gardening in lesser space is vertical gardening. You can use many structures like fences or trellis to make this work. So, what is vertical gardening? Well, it is simple; instead of growing outwards, we grow upwards! If you are someone who has back issues and wants to garden but can't due to the constant bending motion, we've got you covered! So whether you have a patio or a simple backyard, here is how you get started on this rewarding journey.

Vertical gardening is popular due to many reasons. Firstly, you maximize the product. This way, a smaller space guarantees you a forthcoming harvest. It is also physically convenient because there is minimal to no bending. Through vertical gardening, you are making your small space useful.

The spread of disease is also minimized due to the altitude.

Since there is barely any ground contact, you need not worry about the foliage or fruits touching the ground. Furthermore, since the plants are up in the air, circulation is way better, reducing the leftover moisture in the plants, and reducing the probability of any fungus.

One of the most significant factors of photosynthesis is surface area. Being up in the air means that the leaves have a broader surface area for collecting sunlight and hence, more robust growth via better photosynthesis.

Some Plants Like to Climb

Now, not all plants are suited for vertical gardening. For example, plants that tend to vine or sprawl are better suited for vertical plantation.

PERCY SARGEANT

For obvious reasons, plants that grow into bushes are not the best choice. Having a variety of vining plants is a great idea, and they can be set up with the help of a fence or a trellis.

Some of the best options for vertical gardening are as follows:

***"Cherry Tomato*:** Types - 'Sungold', 'Black Cherry', 'Gardener's Delight', and 'Blondkopfchen'

Cucumber: Types - 'Burpee Hybrid II', 'County Fair 83', 'Dasher 11', and 'Saladin'

Green Bean: Types - 'Romano Italian', 'Meraviglia Venezia', and 'Gold of Bacau'

Lima Bean: Types - 'Doctor Martin' and 'King of the Garden'

Melon: Types - 'Delicious 51', 'Tigger', 'Sleeping Beauty' aka musk melon, 'White Wonder', and 'Yellow Doll' aka watermelon

Pea: Types - 'Dual', 'Garden Sweet', 'Maestro', 'Sugar Snap', and 'Super Sugar Snap'

Squash: Types - acorn, delicata, yellow summer, and zucchini" (Create a Vertical Garden for Vegetables, Herbs, and Flowers, 2022).

Now that we have discussed outdoor gardening spaces that allow vegetables to be grown, let us not forget those without any space outside! Many people want to start gardening either for self-sufficiency or just as a hobby but lack any outdoor spaces. These people might live in an apartment building that does not have a garden or backyards available for gardening purposes. This is where indoor gardening comes in. Yes! You can garden indoors using greenhouses.

SMALL INDOOR GREENHOUSE FOR SMALL SPACES

Now, all of you know what a greenhouse is, but how can it be used in indoor gardening?

Did you hear that right, fellas? Indoor gardening isn't only for those who do not have space outside but is also a coveted activity in northern hemisphere regions. People in these regions do not have ample sunlight to grow plants outdoors. These people prefer to build an indoor greenhouse to grow their preferred veggies. With a greenhouse situated indoors, you can start growing your own vegetables.

Many start their seedling growth inside and then plant them outside later. But did you know that you can still grow a plant if you keep those inside and do not transplant them?

I did the same initially and was pleasantly surprised at how well my lettuce plant was growing. No, you do not need any fancy lighting or equipment. Your local everyday fluorescent lights will be enough.

Furthermore, you can plant in pots or any other containers, and it won't even take up too much space of yours! You could do herbs, micro greens, or even full-fledged veggies like peas or broccoli. It is totally up to you!

NEWBIE VEGETABLE CHOICES

However, for first-timers, I would suggest going a little easy on yourself and starting with something easy and convenient. For example, some leafy greens, like kale and arugula, can grow as fast as 4 weeks!

Here is a list of the veggies that are known as cool plants and thrive indoors very nicely:

- "Arugula
- Beets (greens, tiny roots)
- Broccoli (stalks, greens only)
- Brussels Sprouts (stalks, greens only)
- Carrots (tiny but sweet)
- Kale

- Leafy Greens (not head lettuces)

- Mache (corn salad)

- Microgreens (edible seedlings)

- Mustard Greens

- Pea

- Radish

- Sorel

- Spinach

- Swiss chard

- Watercress" (WILL, 2021).

And since we're talking about indoor plants, let us not forget about the herbs. You can grow just about any herb, from basil and mint to thyme, oregano, peppermint, and sage. Plus, let me tell you this: nothing compares to fresh herbs. You might want to stop buying the dried ones from the grocery store after experiencing the taste and aroma of these.

Basic Supplies Needed for Planting and Maintaining Your Small Garden

Indoor gardening is a great option for almost anyone. So, for those of you who are interested, let me list some basic supplies you might need to plant your veggies or herbs. Don't worry. It's nothing fancy. It would be best if you met some conditions for a successful and foolproof indoor plantation, including the light. Since you're indoors, there won't be any sunlight. You may use traditional shop lights that include fluorescent bulbs. These may be used for either starting the seed or for any sort of cool-loving vegetable that you are interested in planting.

On the other hand, for summer or warmth-loving veggies like tomatoes, you might want to opt for the ceramic metal-halide (aka CMH) grow lights. Since indoor gardening is a type of container gardening, you'll need pots and a soilless potting mix for the soil.

You should be wary of the following things while considering, or starting, indoor gardening:

"**Light** – should be low-medium to high, depending on what you're growing

Growing medium – make sure to use organic potting mix for veggies. Try to use containers with drainage holes and saucers or drip trays

Humidity - should range from 40 to 50% for most indoor crops

Water - try and use distilled water if yours is hard or heavy in salts

Air circulation - use an electric fan to help prevent mold and fungus and assist in pollination

Temperature - keep it between 60°F/15°C or 70°F/20°C range depending on the plants

Fertilizer – your soil will need feeding as the plants grow" (WILL, 2021).

GROW A VEGETABLE GARDEN IN POTS AND CONTAINERS

So, this chapter focused on how to start your gardening process. I have covered everything from outdoor and indoor gardening to all the basic supplies you require.

After this, you can decide to initiate your gardening process based on your location and the available space. This was primarily the point of my first chapter; to get you started but with the right option. Now that we have discussed the possibilities of starting the garden, let us move on to the basic structures in our gardening process and how to create the ones I mentioned throughout this chapter.

As I've said before, let's just continue step by step.

Chapter Two

Creative Garden Structures

When it comes to the structure of the kind of containers you wish to have in your garden, it's safe to say that you can use a little creativity. Be bold and experimental. Don't be overwhelmed by the variety of choices of containers. Think of it as an adventure into personal artistic preference. Plus, I'm sure that the plants will love it too. As they say, pretty pot, pretty plant.

As far as the material of your containers is concerned, there is a variety that you can choose from. These include wood, brick, aluminum, plastic, rocks, half-whisky barrel, cinder blocks, milk crates, and concrete blocks. However, knowing there are pros and cons to using each of these materials, what should be a gardener's best choice?

CHOOSE YOUR CONTAINERS WISELY

Since container gardening is literally gardening in a container, you might need to choose your containers wisely. When selecting a suitable container, you need to consider all the aspects of gardening, for example, from climate and light to the kind of space available to you. The material of your container should also be selected with care. From blending in with the space available while looking chic and slick, these containers should also be amicable with your needs as a gardener and the conditions of your location.

Plus, these containers can be in use all year round, so consider them an investment. You don't want to spend your money on new containers every season, now do you?

The first option is the basic terra-cotta containers. These containers are produced in a kiln fire oven and are in colors from orange to creamy pastels. These containers are available in a wide variety of shapes and sizes. They can even be customized if you know anyone who makes them personally. For example, the texture may be smoothed out or left rough for a somewhat rustic look. It can even be designed with embellishments for a fun look.

GROW A VEGETABLE GARDEN IN POTS AND CONTAINERS

The best part about using this container is that the material is porous. That is, air and water can circulate and move in and out of it. However, the same quality sometimes begins to be disadvantageous to the plants. If the material remains dry, terra-cotta sucks the moisture out of the plant's soil and roots, leaving it dehydrated. If not provided with enough moisture, the container itself gets flaky and is prone to more breakage.

Another type of container readily available is a glazed container or pot. These containers are generally made of clay but are later glazed and heated in a kiln to solidify the coating. The finish on the container may be your choice, whether you like a glossy finish or a matte one. You can find them in a range of colors, shapes, and sizes according to your preference. Compared to the terra-cotta ones, these glazed pots are much better at retaining the moisture within the plant and its soil due to the glazing seal. However, the glaze can act as an extra coating and may add to the weight and thickness of the pot. This is especially hard if you want to move the pots around. Plus, if the temperature drops and the air's moisture is less, these pots can dry and become prone to breakage.

The next option is the basic concrete containers. Just like concrete, these can be made into any shape or size, and the finishing can be done according to one's choice. Whether you want some vibrant colors or want to go with an all-natural rustic look. Similar to concrete pots, there is another material known as hypertufa which is very close to what concrete is but is lighter in weight. The pros of keeping concrete containers are obviously their durability. They can last up to a couple of years with minimal care. Their heavy weight reduces any chances you can tip over the container and break it, making them less prone to any breakages. However, the same quality can be a con since the heavier it is, the harder it will be to move around. Plus, just like the rest of the materials, concrete isn't good at surviving freezing cold temperatures and can get dry and wither away.

A xerox copy of concrete is fiber stone. It is an alternative to concrete because it is comparatively lighter in weight. The material is a combination of fiberglass and crushed-up stone. The texture is similar to a rough concrete exterior but is very light in weight and can tolerate extreme temperatures, unlike concrete.

Another primary container material is wood. People who prefer window boxes might find the most options in wooden materials. Some like whiskey barrels, even for wooden window boxes; they look great! The finish can be anything, that is, painted, not painted, sealed, or not sealed. The pros

GROW A VEGETABLE GARDEN IN POTS AND CONTAINERS

of using wooden material for gardening containers are that wood is not affected by harsh freezing temperatures. It is also an excellent insulator and keeps the roots from hot weather in the summer season. One of the most annoying but realistic cons of wooden containers is that wood rots over time. Whether it has come from an expensive bark or a cheap one, it will rot. Even if you seal the surface with your preferred finish, it will need repeated coatings over periods of time.

A non-conventional option is using containers made of cast iron material. Iron can be molded into almost any shape to create a pot of your choice. You can leave it to rust or paint it to your style and preference. The best part about cast iron is that it will last a lifetime. It is a highly durable material. Also, if you live in a location with strong winds, the weight of a cast iron pot will prevent it from falling down or tipping over. However, this weight is disadvantageous if your plants require moving around a lot.

Similar to iron, another material option is sheet metal. Metals like copper, aluminum, and tin can be molded or rolled into sheets to create these pots and containers. One of the most popular choices is "Corten Steel, " a weathered steel type. The advantage of using this material is that it is light in weight and thus can be moved around effortlessly. The material is also quite sturdy and not prone to any cracks or chipping. Even though it is not damaged by extreme weather, like all metals, the intense heat may heat the metal, resulting in the soil drying up too much. Since the steel is thin, dents are inevitable.

We Love Hanging Baskets

Hang in there, fellas!

The one container that some people actually fancy quite a lot is the lined hanging basket that you might have seen swinging over balconies. These baskets are usually made of metal, and the material used for the lining is almost a fibrous one that is either coco fiber or sphagnum moss (DEIKE, 2021). The best part about these fibrous hanging baskets is that they look charming. The neutral color doesn't steal the show but presents your plants prettily. However, the same fiber can look very matte and must be replaced often. Plus, you risk the plant and its soil losing a lot of moisture.

Last but not least comes the obvious choice for most people: plastic and resin. These lookalike materials are mostly copying of ceramic or metal containers and may as well pass for them themselves. However, the actual pots are usually created using either fiberglass, plastic, or resin. The pros of using these containers are their lightweight as well as the durability factor since they can last you a long time. Also, these are weather-resistant, so extreme weather doesn't usually take a toll on them! However, since they might resemble metal or concrete, the truth of the matter is that they aren't the real deal, and their light weight can be troublesome since they can be tipped over easily.

Window Boxes are Chic and Plants Love Them

Now that we have discussed some basic options and their pros and cons, let us detail some of the most popular choices. Number one is window boxes. Now, these containers are easy, convenient, and look so chic! These boxes add so much character to the exterior of your house, on your balconies, and below windows, and can change the look of your home.

BUY CONTAINERS ONLINE OR IN LOCAL STORES

You can find a variety of these window containers in your local nursery or plant shops and even online on Amazon. (Please note: I am going to give you a few specific items I have seen, but I cannot guarantee they will be available when you read this book.) For example, one of the best options is the "Mayne Fairfield Window Box Planter" window box, which is available on Amazon. The container retails for a fairly high price, which may be a bit hefty on the pocket, especially for a plastic container. Trust me, it is worth the hype. The sizes vary, and you can pick the one that suits your style. Its design allows it to water itself, saving you from the effort. The box's material is also UV treated, which prevents the color and appearance from fading away. The best part is that they give you a 15-year warranty! Isn't that cool? The customers at Amazon have also left raving reviews, and most have been granted 5 stars. The material is polythene which allows it to be weather-resistant. You can also choose from various colors, whichever fits your aesthetics. The design creates a water reservoir under the box allowing the plant a self-watering service. This helps you in avoiding frequent watering and saves you the effort.

However, suppose the above box is a little out of your budget. In that case, I have another option for you: "Dynamic Design Newbury Black Resin Window Box." It is comparatively affordable and is available in multiple colors. However, contrary to the "Mayne Fairfield Window Box Planter," the brackets are sold separately and aren't included in the price. The design is pretty basic, but there are multiple colors from which to choose. The resin material makes it durable as well. The best part is that it has a saucer below that collects all the drainage water and ensures that the water doesn't drip down and damage the paint on your wall in case you are hanging it by the window. The material of this box also allows it to be very light in weight; not more than 2 lbs. (0.91 kg) each! Just make sure to purchase some brackets or handles to ensure the box has the support. There are also many available options regarding the size of this particular window box. All in all, this is a great option for value for money and will last you quite some time.

SPLURGE FOR THE BEST DISPLAYS

Now comes the option for all my fancy friends who don't mind splurging a bit: "Veradek Metallic Series Corten Steel Window Box Planter." It is available on Amazon and retails for a whopping $165 US! (at the time of writing this book) Let us see why. It is a very eye-catching design and will look stunning. Although the sizing options are pretty limited, either 48 inches or 36 inches (122 cm or 92cm), the material is solid. These boxes are created from Corten steel, and I have given you all the details. The material is pretty heavy-duty and thick, which is why these boxes are long-lasting and durable, hence, the hefty price. Plus, they have created boxes that grow a rust patina as time passes. This allows them to have a really rustic finish over time. However, as mentioned, it will develop this finish over time. It doesn't come with its signature finish. The best part about these boxes is that they are not prone to any cracks or dents due to the thick Corten steel material. They are also lined with Styrofoam which acts as an insulator and helps prevent the plants from losing moisture, especially in the warmer months of the summer season. They come with drainage holes and stoppers as well. A point to keep in mind is that you will need to purchase any additional tools to mount it up separately since the box doesn't include it. Overall, these boxes are expensive but durable, so it depends on whether you can afford them.

The best option for any self-watering box is a window box known as "Gardener's Supply Self-Watering Window Box." All the boxes mentioned, including this one, are available at multiple online outlets like Amazon. This one, for starters, is for those of my plant parent friends who often forget to water their plants or those who simply don't want to frequently take out the time and go water their babies. This box has a self-watering system that allows the plants to remain happy and healthy without having you fuss over the process. The material, even though it is plastic, is frost resistant. The colors available, though, are only two: classic terra cotta and white. Basic, I know, but they go with almost anything. So, if you want to keep it minimalistic, these are great options. The size is excellent and allows about 28 quarts (26.5 liters) of soil, while the water tank can hold up to 9 quarts (8.5 liters) of water which is enough to keep your plants hydrated. You can even check the water level since it offers a convenient scale. Contrary to the previous option, this window box has brackets to mount it up for support, so you don't have to purchase them separately. Something to keep in mind is that as the season changes, you might want to avoid any standing water left in the reservoir because if you experience extreme winters, the water could freeze up, leaving your plants struggling and dying.

Now that we have discussed some basic examples of window boxes and where to buy them let us move on to the other type of containers. Obviously, window boxes aren't the only options for the plantation of your veggies or whatever it is that you plan on planting. The best part about using containers or different planters for growing your vegetables is that you do not need a lot of space for these. It is productive as well as gorgeous to look at. You can construct many planters that fit your aesthetic.

Be Bold – Choose Colorful Pots! Create a Statement!

Something that people always go for is bright and colorful pots! You can literally use containers or pots made up of any material mentioned above in different colors. The finish could be glossy or matte, whichever you prefer. Glazed pots are all the rage these days, and people get them in all sorts of pastels or vibrant and loud colors to add some color to their gardens. Another option is to use those raised baskets that I talked about earlier. So, what if you do not have a lot of ground space in your abode? Hang those plants! Veggies and herbs grow very nicely in these compacted or bush-hanging baskets and look equally pretty. Pair some tomatoes with basil. The pair creates a stunning look, and you will have some Caprese salad at hand.

Something that a lot of people like to do, especially for the sake of today's environment and with the cloud of climate change looming over our heads, is recycling old or used containers! Yes, you can literally use any leftover containers in your house to plant your vegetables. Use those old wine bottles and plant that lettuce you want for your Caesar salad. Save money as well as the environment.

If you really want to have that eye-catching feature in your garden, then don't shy away from creating differences in it. Play with the heights and colors of your pots. Don't have a monotonous tone to your garden. Add that visual interest by having different-sized containers. A small and broad one for your bushel of tomatoes and perhaps a tall and skinny one for your herbs like parsley or thyme. Create a dynamic look. Similarly, experiment with the color as well. Instead of only focusing on colorful pots, grow those colorful veggies too. And why only vegetables? Grow some easy flowers! Do a little marigold alongside your red and green peppers. Oh, how they will create some striking colors! Plus, you can even plant edible flowers and add color to not only your garden but to your plate as well! Edible flowers are great with desserts as well as salads. From pansies and calendula to honeysuckles, the options are endless!

Play with textures and create a statement! For example, have some thyme planted next to your eggplant. The thorny and pointy look of your thyme leaves will contrast with the large flat leaves of the eggplant plant and create a rustic look. Similarly, add texture with some ornamental grass. Plant some lemongrass or even some chives to create that aesthetic look for your garden. Basically, grass on its own enhances the look of the rest of your plants and pops them out even more since it creates a base.

One thing that I would suggest to everyone is that don't shy away from vining plants. They may come off intimidating since the general ones like watermelon or even pumpkin require a lot of space, but there are options that grow in a container perfectly fine. Cucumbers grow on vines and create a stunning landscape in your garden with their beautiful large leaves. You can even look into lemon cucumbers for that extra color! But, to plant these vining plants, you must aid them with some support like a trellis so they can climb onto it. Cucumbers can be supported upright. Bamboo stakes are also great for holding your plants.

Moving on, let us discuss some options for those raised beds! You can get creative with your raised beds in so many ways. The best part about having or creating raised beds is that they can be a permanent place for your plants to grow and mature. From your price point, raised beds depend on how you want them. Obviously, the more complex you build them, the more expensive it gets, but once you've created them, they don't cost more than your regular garden in terms of maintenance.

Custom Design or Buy Ready Built Beds

The first option is to custom-design your own raised beds. Whatever space you have in your garden doesn't matter because you can create your own design that utilizes that space. You can get the landscaping done according to your design or something you have seen in a picture. For example, you could add a section for a bench or seating where you can just sit and admire your garden.

Another option is to avoid the hassle of custom designing and get the built-in ones instead. They may cost you more, but it saves the work and effort of building them yourself. Plus, they're easy and convenient, especially if you don't fancy yourself as a handy person. You can place these wherever you feel that your plants will get the optimal conditions to thrive and mature successfully. Raised beds are all the rage due to the fact that you can literally control the conditions like the soil as well as the water drainage. This ensures that your plants turn out the way you want them to. Plus, if you have any back issues and can't afford all the bending, raised beds are a great idea since they are raised!

Many people go for metal as a material for their raised beds. Metal is vulnerable to temperature, whether it's hot or cold. Apart from the typical metal raised beds, you can even go for the grow bags. They prevent the soil from freezing and defrosting in the winter season. Similarly, they can provide optimal heat for your plants. They are a terrific option for growing all those plants that need heat, like Mediterranean plants, including mint and chives. Oh, how they love themselves some sun!

Raised bed ideas include the option of square gardening. This means that you divide your garden area into square feet (or meters). This allows you to be highly productive with your space and have a fruitful garden. Similarly, you create the raised beds per square foot (square meter) and garden accordingly. All in all, there are many options for using raised beds in your garden, including the ones I have mentioned.

Simple Tools for Gardening

Now that we have discussed all the structures that you might opt for depending on your preferences for your garden, including the materials used for them, let us talk about some basics like the tools that you require to garden, take care of your plants, and also to lay out the structures you want. You need some basic gardening supplies to start everything. First and foremost comes the soil. Soil isn't just the dirt you think it is. It is the medium where your plant will thrive and derives all its nutrients.

The next step is to get some tools. You need a gardening hoe to prep your soil and also to remove any existing weeds. There are plenty of options in terms of sizes and colors but choose one that fits perfectly and feels easy to use. Get a gardening rake. This is essential for vegetable gardening since you will need to clear out the soil from those dead leaves and foliage.

GROW A VEGETABLE GARDEN IN POTS AND CONTAINERS

A shovel is next. You need to dig, and you need something sharp and effective, so look for the ones that have this quality. A gardening trowel is also necessary. Individual plants or seeds are not something that can be handled with a shovel. Small gardening tasks require a trowel. However, you don't want to get your hands dirty when you use all these, so some gardening gloves are a must! So, invest in a good pair. You might even need different ones depending on other types of gardening tasks.

Moreover, don't forget their most essential tool: the water source. Your plants need that water. From cans to hoses, pick anything depending on the size of your garden. These are some basic tools you must obtain to start your gardening endeavor; honestly, they are more than enough since you are just beginning. You don't need to invest in any fancy equipment just yet.

Overall, this chapter has discussed in detail all the options you have to start the plantation process. I have touched on everything from window boxes to containers and all the materials and their pros and cons. You even have the option to directly order your boxes since I have given you examples of some of the best-sellers to save you the hassle. Now that we have, in fact, talked about the kind of containers that you might need to start your garden; whether you prefer pots and window boxes or you want to construct your own raised beds, let us now move on to the more exciting part: choosing the best kind of vegetables that you can grow since you want to initiate your small space gardening.

Chapter Three

Vegetable Choices and Regional Gardens

When approaching the art of small-space gardening, many people are pretty apprehensive about it. They feel that the vegetables they like to eat and those they are allowed to grow in their respective climate conditions are mutually exclusive.

That might be true, but only to some extent. In the US, every region is different from another. So many time differences in the same country mean that, obviously, the climate conditions also differ from one another. But that doesn't mean that you just cannot grow the food that you would like to eat. In fact, the book's very essence, especially what I mentioned at the very start, is to grow something you would like to eat for yourself or what your family enjoys consuming. What is the point of having a vegetable neither you nor your family likes to eat?

There is no joy in gardening and putting in the effort if you won't be consuming the fruit or, much to the point, vegetables of your labor.

This book primarily aims at those who do not have enough space to start a full-scale garden. Hence, the name "small space." This is precisely why I have touched upon the various ways to utilize the small space: use pots and containers if you have hard surfaces or platforms, and use raised garden beds if you have proper gardening space.

There are plenty of vegetables that you can grow in the US in either of these options. We have discussed the various types, advantages, and disadvantages of raised beds and different pots and containers.

Annual and Perennial What's the Difference?

Firstly, you must select or differentiate between perennial and annual plants before choosing your veggies. Welcome to garden basics 101. Don't get too overwhelmed skimming through a seed booklet and not knowing the meaning of perennial and annual seeds. I've got you covered.

Overall, this is all you need to know regarding the annuals and the perennials. An annual plant is one that grows for a single season and then is done for. However, a perennial plant tends to grow for more than one season.

Born and Growing in the USA

Let us analyze what to actually grow, especially if you are living in the US. Whether you have raised beds or containers, it doesn't matter because these veggies can grow in both!

GROW A VEGETABLE GARDEN IN POTS AND CONTAINERS

First, some carrots. Now, carrots are a staple veggie for any stock or sauce. Take Bolognese, for example. Since carrot is a root vegetable, a raised bed is a fine option since it offers space and aeration.

Mostly, certain types of carrots are grown in different circumstances. The seeds are very small and do not need a lot of water; a ¼ inch (0.64cm) in depth is more than enough, so don't overdo it! Still, a regular carrot can be planted in a square foot of space, and you can grow 18 of them simultaneously.

Next up is the American salad staple: kale. Kale is a favorite from the salad queen, Kourtney Kardashian, to your local salad bar. Just like the rest of the veggies, a single kale plant will need a square foot (30 square centimeters) of space, and since it is a leafy green, it prefers cool shade. You could plant it next to your eggplant since it could provide some shade with its huge leaves. Whether you want to start from the kale seeds or transplant the kale, it's your choice.

Cucumbers are also a popular option among home gardeners. The first step is to choose either a bush or a vining one. But whichever you choose, get a trellis to help it climb. Plant them close to the trellis, and be sure to keep them 6 feet away from each other while ensuring they are planted more than an inch deep into the soil. This way, you will spot the veggie easily when it grows.

Another excellent kitchen staple is lettuce. It is such a convenient vegetable that you can grow it almost anywhere, especially in those nooks and crannies that seem out of the way in your garden. It proliferates quickly and can be planted near a large plant, like tomatoes, since it loves the shade. The seeds are tiny, so don't drown them in water. Plant them in straight lines and cover them gently with soil.

Next up are radishes. Yes, these spicy veggies are a gardener's dream. They are fast-growing and can mature in as little as 20 days! Simply dig a small trench and sprinkle your seeds before carefully covering them with soil. Water gently, and you're done!

The ideal neighbor for your radishes is spinach. Spinach grows best in cool weather, so start early. Plant it just like you plant your lettuce. Don't thin out the spinach as you do with kale and lettuce. Baby spinach is equally yummy, nutritious, and great for consumption.

Last but not least is tomatoes. Italian dinner nights are not just possible without tomatoes. Especially if you have fresh and homegrown tomatoes at hand, trust me, there is nothing better. From heirlooms to cherry tomatoes, these juicy fruits (yes, fruits) are a staple in your kitchen. Want to whip up a quick snack? Make a quick salsa with tomatoes, onions, and some jalapenos. Tomatoes can grow with or without a trellis, although a plant hiked up on a lattice looks truly stunning. Start your seeds around 2 feet

(0.61 meters) apart and let them grow into beautiful ripe red tomatoes. Or, if you want to do something a little fancy, try a Caprese salad!

These are just some plants you can grow in your home garden. Others include cucamelons, summer squash, peas, beans, celery, onions, peppers, beets, arugula, swiss chard, zucchinis, and even patty pans!

And let us not forget the herbs; these are an absolute must in a home garden since they can elevate any dish. And trust me when I say this, fresh is always better than dry. You can plant basil, thyme, oregano, rosemary, and even mint! I mean, how else are you going to make your gorgeous Caprese salad?

Planting Vegetables at Home in Australia

Now, I want to focus on the kind of vegetables that are ideally grown in different parts of the world, especially in home gardening. Let us start with Australia. Even though the country is enormous and the temperatures are extreme, a variety of vegetables grow very well in this region.

First up is the infamous swiss chard. It is one of the most convenient vegetables to grow in Australia since it doesn't require too much sunlight and doesn't die if left unwatered.

Next up are cherry tomatoes.

PERCY SARGEANT

Cherry tomatoes love some sun, and if you don't plan on damaging the plant before the harvest, you're in it to win it! Control your urge to remove them even if they don't look quite right or are tangled. They'll get through it themselves.

And do not trim it! Trim it, and you'll most definitely kill it. The key is not to plant too many at the same time.

Another great option is to plant some spring onions. The best part about spring onions is that if you keep leaving in the roots and trim the green part for yourself, they will keep growing back and last you a great while!

If you're an avid salad eater, planting some lettuce and other leafy greens is something you can do to add some freshness! As mentioned before, lettuce grows very fast. They grow even faster in the hot weather, which means that you will have to harvest them equally fast; otherwise, they will wither.

If you like yourself a nice ratatouille, consider planting an eggplant plant. Basically, in a nutshell, tomatoes and eggplants are like cousins. They not only go well together, but they also like the same things.

For example, both grow nicely in warmer weather and need support. So, install some stakes for the eggplants since the veggies grow somewhat heavy. Be sure to feed and water your plants well and leave the rest to them.

Next up are beetroots. No, you don't have to buy canned beets anymore. These veggies grow all year round, making them perfect for Australia and any country!

Plus, you could use the leaves for your salad. Such a productive vegetable, right?

Don't forget the new staple vegetable that is zucchini. Zucchini comes in a variety of shapes, sizes, and even colors. You can eat its flowers by using them in salads or as a garnish.

So, that was it for a little visit to Australia. Let us move a little west in the northern hemisphere by landing in the center of Europe, specifically choosing Germany as an exemplar of vegetable growing in their climate.

German Favorites

It is important for me to create awareness regarding the planting of vegetables in the rest of the world since it is not only people in the US who are reading this book. We just talked about Australia, so now let us discuss the German gardening basics. We can discuss the best vegetables to grow in Germany by moving through the seasons. Let me start by giving you guys some examples.

For starters, summer ranges from June to August, while winters move from December to February. Meanwhile, spring lasts from March to May; autumn starts in September and fades away in November.

As far as the popular summer veggies are concerned, then asparagus tops the list. You can plant crowns to fasten the asparagus' growth process for an earlier harvest.

Plant them 8 to 12 inches (20 to 30cm) apart and water them generously by covering almost 2 inches (5 centimeters) of the ground. Asparagus might appear a bit dry when you look at it, so it is vital to soak it in water for at least 2 hours before planting it. Make sure to water it enough for it not to struggle.

Another awesome summer plant is squash. You can either start the process directly in the soil outside or indoors.

When it comes to the winter season, you have probably the most popular veggie option: potatoes. Contrary to popular opinion, the potato is a humble, no-frills plant and is not complicated. All it needs is well-drained soil as a medium to grow. The best time for the harvest is when it is wintertime. Plus, you should wait for the foliage to settle down and fade away. Once that is out of the way, your plant will be done, and you will have nice round potatoes to make some French fries or even a potato salad if you wish.

As far as the fall season is concerned, spinach is a great choice. It loves a combination of sun and shade.

It is safe to say that any green leafy vegetables can be grown in Germany in the fall season. Swiss chard is a good option to grow as a fall vegetable, and so is lettuce. This list also includes radishes and peas.

Tropical Divas

Since we are talking about the different kinds of vegetables that grow worldwide, let us discuss some vegetables that are ideal for tropical weather, which is humid and hot.

Vegetables that grow in the United States, such as tomatoes and lettuce, are not suited to the hot and humid climate of the tropics. Indeed, these temperature conditions aren't the most suitable for plants since they can trigger any type of disease or even pests. However, that doesn't mean that rainy areas cannot cultivate any kind of vegetables whatsoever. Leafy green veggies are not the best choice since they love their coolness and shade. Too much heat will cause them to wilt. Let's be honest; who likes soggy and wilted vegetables?

The tropics are renowned for their bugs and insects. Of course, there are insects in every part of the world, especially in gardens. Still, the tropical climate really allows them to thrive. Hence, they are notorious for ruining plants.

So, it is important that your plants grow happy and healthy, and therefore must be grown in good quality soil that provides them with all the optimal conditions to supply them with happiness rather than leaving them struggling on their own. This way, they will be less susceptible to insects and any other pests.

Any plant that does not agree with the hot and humid climate conditions will struggle to grow. Eventually, it will become weak and die. These plants are most prone to bugs and diseases. So, it is crucial for you to plant those vegetables and plants that can thrive in tropical climates.

Now let me give you some examples of the vegetables you can grow if you live in a tropical area. Tomatoes like to grow there, provided you plant them in the winter season. If you plant them in the rainy season, there is no chance they will give you a successful harvest. Shocker, yes, but it is the truth.

Plus, you need to make sure to choose a variety that has a good heat tolerance too. For example, choose cherry tomatoes instead of going for regular plum tomatoes. They are hardier and have a better chance of growing in a rainy and humid environment.

Furthermore, don't bother yourself by attempting to plant your salad greens. All that kale, lettuce, and arugula won't survive the heat and humidity, and all your efforts will be in vain. Instead, go for the Asian greens. Try planting some Chinese or regular cabbage.

GROW A VEGETABLE GARDEN IN POTS AND CONTAINERS

You can also try and plant typical tropical vegetables like sweet potatoes. Now, sweet potatoes love the heat and the wet season and will grow so much that they might even overcrowd your garden.

Suppose you are adamant about planting some greens. In that case, you could go for kang kong, known as water spinach, amaranth, which is similar to spinach, and salad mallow (Grant, 2021).

More options for tropical veggies are as follows:

"Bamboo Shoot | Chaya Chayote | Climbing Wattle | Cowpea | Cucumber | Eggplant | Vegetable Fern | Jack Bean | Katuk Leaf Pepper | Long Bean | Malabar Spinach | Mustard Greens | Okra | Pumpkin | Roselle | Scarlet Ivy Gourd | Sunn Hemp (a legume cover crop) | Sweet Potato | Tropical/Indian Lettuce | Wax Gourd/Winter Melon | Winged Bean" Grant, 2021).

Some veggies are more suited to growing in the winter or when there is less dryness. This also includes bitter gourd melon Calabash Angled luffa, which is very much like zucchini.

Now that I have listed all the plants and vegetable ideal for growing in the rainy and humid season let's move on to the drier side of life, the deserts.

Desert not Dessert

Most people I have come across are under the impression that deserts are only good for a plant like the cactus and aren't conducive to a garden or growing other plants and vegetables.

On the contrary, this is an absolutely wrong assumption! Yes, deserts feature high temperatures and little rainfall. Still, they can be home to different plants and flowers (even edible ones if you like). As in the rest of the world, you must consider your type of soil, its nutrition, and other climate conditions such as water and light.

Firstly, you need to get your soil tested. You may use some soilless pot mix or some organic stuff for its nutrition. However, the ideal option is to actually get your soil tested. The critical nutrients for any plant's growth include nitrogen, phosphorus, and potassium. These are also some of the elemental chemical compositions in fertilizers. The exact amount of all these nutrients solely depends on the type of plant you are choosing to grow.

Desert soil is already notorious for its high salt levels. It is advised not to use regular manure since it has a high percentage of salt. However, you have to make sure that these vegetables, plants, or flowers need come under the category of "non-drought tolerant desert plants."

GROW A VEGETABLE GARDEN IN POTS AND CONTAINERS

As far as the light is concerned, you get plenty of it in the desert! You might even get more than the regular 6 to 8 hours. But since the desert offers an extreme amount of light, it is better to opt for plants having thick skin. So, choose wisely since you don't want your plants to burn or dry out.

The next most important thing to keep in mind is the water situation. Remember, these are desert plants, and they get mighty thirsty. Make sure to water at least 2 inches (5 centimeters) every day.

Now, let me give you a sampling of those vegetables you can successfully grow in the desert environment.

For the cool season, the options are these fellas:

"Beet
Broccoli
Cabbage
Carrot
Lettuce
Onion
Pea
Potato
Radish
Spinach
Turnip" (Grant, 2012)

Options for the warmer months include,

"Bean
Cucumber
Eggplant
Melon

PERCY SARGEANT

Pepper
Pumpkin
Squash
Corn
Sweet Potato
Tomato" (Grant, 2021).

That being said, if you live in the desert region and you don't have the space for outdoor gardening, then perhaps you might choose to grow indoors, and there are numerous options for indoor plantations. These include scallions, radishes, potatoes, spinach, tomatoes, strawberries, herbs, and even microgreens! All the basic types of equipment and containers have been highlighted in the previous chapter, so I will list what you can start growing.

Overall, this chapter has highlighted a number of options you have for the vegetables and plants that you might prefer to garden. From lettuce to tomatoes to eggplants and even edible flowers like pansies, there are many possibilities for home gardening.

Furthermore, I have talked about not just the vegetables you can grow in the US but also in other parts of the world. So far, we have debated over the two opposite countries on the globe; Australia and Germany, that is, from the southern hemisphere to the northern hemisphere and from the tropics to the deserts.

So, gardening is always an option wherever you are in the world.

Next up, we are touching on the details of soil and some of the basics you need to know about the type of plants suited for specific types of soil.

GROW A VEGETABLE GARDEN IN POTS AND CONTAINERS

I will also discuss the joy of creating your own compost and its magical properties.

Chapter Four

Soil Science Basics and Composting Magic

Let us start with the most repeated question: why is soil so important?

The most straightforward answer to this question is that soil is the medium in which plants grow. From essential nutrients to basic necessities, like water and air, soil provides them to your plant. It is also to be noted that each area has its own soil chemistry. Each soil is different, from nutrients and minerals to organic and inorganic materials. That is precisely why different types of plants thrive in other areas and locations.

You might relate to this since we discussed all the climates in the previous chapter. You may also recall the details about the areas prone to different types of vegetable growth and how certain vegetables do not grow competently in other regions.

If, for example, you want to grow a specific plant, but the soil conditions do not align with the plant's needs, you might be a little bummed. However, that is why there are containers and raised beds.

A Lesson in Creating Your Own Soil!

Basically, there are a total of six types of soils on this earth. These include clay, sandy, silty, peaty, chalky, and loamy. Each has different characteristics that make them suitable for various plants and vegetables.

Clay

Let us start with the clay soil. Clay soil is rock hard when it turns dry but super sticky if wet. It has poor drainage due to these properties. It may be rich in nutrients and minerals, but the drainage issue doesn't grow your plants nicely.

However, if you try to improve its drainage, it is an excellent medium for plants. Some of the plants that can grow in this soil include perennial plants. We have discussed previously what perennial plants are. For example, they include tomatoes, mango, coconut, etc. Shrubs are also grown in clay soil. These range from Helen's flower and aster to bergamot and flowering quince (Barton, 2022). Basically, summer plants are a comparatively good option for clay soils. Trees, especially, thrive in this soil. On the other hand, soft berry plants are not a good option, so don't try and plant those.

Sandy

Next up is the sandy soil. Physically, this soil feels quite gritty but has excellent drainage since it dries out fairly quickly. It is easy to cultivate but lacks nutrients. So ideally, you should amend it by manually adding in some manure like glacial rock dust, greensand, and kelp meal. Basically, the key is to add any other that is available to you.

Like clay soil, shrubs are an excellent option to grow in sandy soil. These include tulips, tree mallow, sun roses, and hibiscus.

You have options to grow vegetables as well. The preferred ones include root vegetables like beets, parsnips, potatoes, or even carrots. Some of the most popular vegetables for sandy soil (especially commercially) include lettuce, strawberries, peppers, corn, squash, zucchini, collard greens, and tomatoes (Barton, 2022).

Silty

The third type of soil is silty soil. This soil is known to feel somewhat soapy, as strange as it sounds. It is also very soft to the touch. However, regardless of its strange characteristics, it is excellent at retaining moisture and nutrients. It is effortless to cultivate and doesn't require a lot of labor. The drainage system might be questioned, but add a little compost or organic matter and trust me, you're sorted.

Like the rest of the soils, shrubs, like silty soil, grow pretty well. Alongside these, so do perennial plants, grasses, and climbers.

Trees are also a great option. You could even try and plant willow, birch, dogwood, and cypress since they like the moisture property of the silty soil.

Regarding vegetables and plants, most vegetables and fruits thrive in this soil since they provide excellent optimal conditions.

Peaty

Next on the list is peaty soil. Its consistency is quite spongy and damp. the peat also contributes to its dark color. The soil has lower nutrient levels because it is acidic, so the decomposition process is relatively slow. It retains water, and the drainage isn't ideal. However, the acidic levels can be reduced by neutralizing them with limestone or mixing in some organic compost material.

Plants and vegetables that do well in peaty soils are as follows: "shrubs (heather, lantern trees, witch hazel, camellia, rhododendron, and azalea) and vegetable such as Brassicas, legumes, root crops as well as salad crops since they thrive in well-drained peaty soils" (Barton, 2022).

Chalky

The fifth type is called chalky soil. Much like its name, the soil is stony and has larger particles than the rest. Due to its alkaline nature, plants usually struggle a lot and end up with pale leaves that are almost yellow in color. However, you can always solve the pH issue by adding an acidic fertilizer and ending up with some neutral soil. Hummus is a great option and is known to reduce alkaline levels, as well as enhance drainage.

These vegetables can easily be grown in chalky soil: **spinach, beets, sweet corn, and cabbage** (Barton, 2022).

Loamy

The next type of soil is called loamy soil. This soil is a mixture of some of the above soils: silty, sand, and clay. The texture is relatively smooth, and it is pretty damp.

These characteristics make it an ideal medium for growing plants, shrubs, vegetables, flowers, etc. The drainage is also pretty standard. It retains the mixture quite well and also has a lot of nutrients.

Furthermore, even though it warms up quickly as the spring season arrives, it doesn't lose its moisture or dry out in summer heat. It is more on the acidic side of the scale if you ever get the chance to check its pH value. But all that can be sorted out by regularly adding some organic material, or compost, to the soil.

Now, there is plenty that you can grow in this soil, from perennials and shrubs to tubers like wisteria, dog's-tooth violets, rubus, and delphinium. Due to its productive nature, it is an ideal medium for almost all berry crops and veggies.

Although it is prone to drying out, make sure to focus on rotating the crops as well as feeding the soil as much compost and organic matter as possible to ensure that it is rich in nutrients.

As we have discussed previously, the best part about small-space gardening is the fact that you can use different containers or raised beds to start your plantation process.

This means that instead of making do with the soil present in your garden, you can literally go and buy a soil mix you prefer that will yield the best possible results for your plants. So go and visit your nearest gardening store and buy a mix. And boom! You're all done from the soil point of view.

When using raised beds for gardening, the soil tends to stay loose and uncompacted since there are fewer chances of you or anyone else stepping on it. This is another one of the advantages of using raised beds.

Best Choice: Loam

The question that might arise after this is, what is the best soil to use? From what you have read above and what I have gathered, loam is the ideal choice.

Potting Mix

As mentioned before, you can get a soilless mix from your local gardening shop. This potting comprises mixed ingredients explicitly for container gardening and raised beds. The name "black dirt" is also sometimes referred to as "topsoil."

A good potting mix always contains organic material such as peat, moss, compost, or even bark. Other ingredients include vermiculite or perlite. These ensure that the soil retains its moisture. Since these mixes are usually made from topsoil, they contain sand, limestone, and other nutrients. Some of the blends may even be made by combining fertilizers. You can read the packaging of your mixes before buying them to get a better idea. This is because you need to know what is in your potting mix to ensure that it is the best option for your plants.

As I have mentioned numerous times before, when growing your plants, you must strengthen your soil with organic material. Whether the soil is organic or not, it can monumentally affect your plant's growth.

Organic & Inorganic

Organic and inorganic soils differ in terms of what the soil contains. For example, inorganic soil mainly contains synthetic fertilizers, pesticides, and soil amendments. This ensures the prevention of diseases and protection from insects and pests.

On the other hand, organic soil is composed chiefly of similar non-synthetic and natural materials. These range from compost, mulch, and manure to soil amendments.

The term "organic" has grown to be more prevalent in recent years and is one of the reasons for the increase in home gardening. The basis for this is that organic soil is free of any chemicals. This makes it better for plants as well as the environment, and, besides, food grown in these soils provides you with better health possibilities.

As far as the cost of soil is concerned, a bag of topsoil typically ranges from 2 to 5 US dollars (at the time of writing this book) and contains 40 lbs (18 kgs) for every cubic foot. It is simple if you want to budget out the cost but don't know how much soil you need. All you need to do is measure the area you need to fill with your soil. This could be your raised beds, containers, or a yard. By measuring the length, width, and depth, you can calculate the area and, subsequently, the volume. You will get an answer in cubic feet or meters and get the required amount.

The United States Agricultural Department has a federal regulatory program that develops and enforces consistent national standards for organically produced agricultural products sold in the United States. It is known as the national organic program (NOP). The NOP accredited third-party organizations to certify that farms and businesses meet the national organic standards. Plus, these certifiers, and USDA, work together to enforce the standards, ensuring a level playing field for producers and protecting consumer confidence (National Organic Program | Agricultural Marketing Service, n.d.).

Plants Love Organic Compost

Since I have constantly mentioned the substance "compost" and how it is nutritious for plants, let me elaborate on this material. Compost basically consists of decaying organic matter. Generally speaking, compost can be made out of any vegetative matter. For example, the materials used for compost are veggie food scraps, lawn clippings, and leaves.

Beautiful Compost and its Benefits

Compost is used due to the many benefits it has for the soil. It increases the nutrients in your soil and improves its drainage. Due to beneficial bacteria and microbes, adding compost allows your plants to be vigorous and tolerate stress better. It also enhances the taste of food, including vegetables. All in all, compost boosts the health and vitality of plants. Since compost is acidic, it can help balance out the pH of your soil if it is alkaline. Similarly, the addition of compost can cause the soil to turn acidic. Thus, you might need to add some limestone to neutralize it. The great thing about compost is that it is essentially free of cost. Just use all the leftovers you have!

GROW A VEGETABLE GARDEN IN POTS AND CONTAINERS

START COMPOSTING!

Now, how to start composting? The first step is to create your compost by laying it out on the bare earth. This ensures the worms or other organisms transport it to your garden as well as aerate it.

Next, make sure to first lay down some twigs a few inches deep. This will improve drainage. The most important part is to lay out the compost in layers. Alternate between the wet and dry.

For example, the moist compost comprises tea bags and food scraps. The dry ones range from draws, leaves, wood ashes, etc. In addition to this, add some manure as a nitrogen source. This will activate your compost. It will also ensure that your compost is moist, so water it accordingly. For the sake of its moisture, try and keep it covered. You can utilize any material, for example, a sheet. This will retain the moisture and prevent any drying. Also, after every few weeks, turn the pile to aerate it. You can also keep on adding material by mixing it in. it won't be necessary for you to keep layering afterward.

Basically, this is how you start composting yourself. You can always get a composter if you don't want to exert too much effort. Getting a ready-made composter obviously saves you the hassle and the time. Let us start with choosing a composter.

There are three things that you must consider before buying one:

- Where you live
- What materials you'll be composting
- Whether you want to manually turn your compost or not

I'll address the general majority. Most of us who want to garden live in either urban or suburban areas and have access to gardens, backyards, or any other outdoor space. Hence, the majority of the materials for composting will consist mainly of composting mainly kitchen scraps, with some yard waste. The best option is to get either a worm bin or a compost tumbler.

COMPOST CONTAINER OPTIONS

There are a lot of containers available for composting. For small-space composting, you can choose from DIY compost bins and compost digesters to tumblers.

The DIY bin is the least expensive and can be done in a garbage can. All you have to do is drill some holes. Follow the steps I have mentioned above, and boom! You've started your own small-scale composting.

The next option is to get a compost bin or digester. These are closed from the top and the sides while being open at the bottom. This allows them to sit directly on the ground. The pro about these bins is that they are inexpensive.

However, turning is difficult since they sit on top of the compost. This prolongs the composting process. Plus, the bins are plastic and can chip or break easily.

The most sustainable and efficient option is to buy yourself a tumbler. Since it is an enclosed bin, It behaves like an insulator, and the temperature is easy to maintain. This keeps the microbes in the compost active. Each design varies to aid the composting process. For example, some have holes at the bottom to help with the aeration.

The benefits of using a tumbler for composting are as follows:

- It speeds up the composting process

- The composts last year-round owing to the warm internal temperature

- Rodents, raccoons, dogs, or other critters cannot access it since it is enclosed

- The enclosed design keeps the compost secure and odor-free, making it well-suited for residential areas and large apartment terraces or patios (Composting: How to Make Compost Using Tumblers & Bins, n.d.).

In addition to the ones mentioned above, some fancy composting containers tumble the ingredients. You may also find some stainless-steel containers with charcoal filters that can be used inside the kitchen. Some options include ones made of heavy, recycled plastic that can handle 3 to 300 gallons (11 to 1135 liters) of compost material. Overall, there are many choices; some are expensive, while others are not. The cheap options include the DIY and standard bins.

Composting from Scratch

If you are really interested in building your compost bin from scratch, here are two different methods on how to build one using much the same material. The first is very simple and inexpensive, while the other involves more effort, a little more money, and the aid of an assistant. This one gives you more access, employing a "door" to tend to the material inside. Make sure to choose a place with ample sunlight and heat. This is essential to speed up the composting process

Number 1 - The Simple Compost Bin

You will need a few items to build this bin:

- Wire mesh hardware cloth

- Hammer

- Gloves

- Protective glasses

Follow these steps to build a cylindrical compost bin:

1. The compost bin should be at least 3 feet (0.9 meters) in diameter. A three-foot (0.92 meters) wide compost bin requires 10 feet (3 meters) of wire fencing. A four-foot wide bin requires 12 1/2 feet (3.8 meters) of fencing

2. Cut the fencing with wire cutters or tin snips. Make sure to cut the cross wires carefully, so there are no sharp ends sticking out. Remember to wear gloves! The cut wire can be very sharp.

3. To stop the fencing from curving, open it on the ground and walk over it to flatten it. This will make it easier to handle. Then, form a cylinder with the mesh wire.

4. You can use wire, twine, or zip ties to fasten it. Make sure the compost bin is secure by fastening the ends at the top, middle, and bottom.

5. Just make sure you have enough room to move around it. for those times when you need to turn it or harvest the compost.

NUMBER 2 - THE LESS SIMPLE COMPOST BIN

The second one is a larger compost container and might be a little too elaborate for your needs, but nevertheless, allow me to give you a few tips on its construction in case it could be of interest to you. This one has a "door" you can open to get to the compost material, allowing you to mix it up.

Here are the supplies you will need: (you will also need an assistant)

- 4 metal T-posts (or wooden)
- Wire mesh fencing, also known as hardware cloth (14ft x 4 1/2 ft) (1.2m x 1.37m)
- Baling wire
- Tape measure
- Hammer
- Gloves
- Protective glasses

GROW A VEGETABLE GARDEN IN POTS AND CONTAINERS

Note: These supplies and tools apply to a 3ft x 3ft (0.91m x 0.91m) area. However, this can be flexible according to the space you have.

Constructing the square compost enclosure:

1. Begin by driving in your number 1 T-post (metal T-posts are sturdier than wooden ones) with the help of a hammer, forming a square with each pole at the corner measuring 3 feet (1 meter) apart – adjust according to your space.

2. Make sure it feels nice and sturdy since it will be providing you with most of the support, and set up all 4 of them in the area you have decided.

3. Make sure to wear gloves to protect your hands from the sharp edges of the mesh cloth.

4. Cut off a foot of baling wire and fasten the mesh to post number 1 - thread it through the mesh, twist the wire, snip the sharp ends off, and repeat in 3 places down the T-post.

5. Make a fence by wrapping the wire mesh cloth around the other 3 T-posts bringing it back to post number 1.

6. Secure the other 2 T-posts in the same way with the baling wire.

7. Cut off the excess mesh leaving an extra 6 inches past the number 4 T-post to be used as a "door." Fold over the end about an inch or more so there are no sharp edges.

8. Use a simple clip attached to the mesh side to keep the "door'

closed.

Here is how to treat the compost material:

- Layer, then water, and repeat it. After being done with that, just mix and cover

- Turn every 3 days

- Check the temperature; it needs to heat up as hot as possible

- In colder climates, it will take longer for the temperature to rise

- Use a compost thermometer (about $20 US), at the time of writing this book, or just put metal rebar in and touch the skin - leave the thermometer in the pile

- What is making it steam? Microbial activity and a reasonable rate of decomposition. It can reach up to 140°F. (60°C). 120°F (49°C) is the perfect temperature

- Mix compost by moving inside to outside

- Wait 3 weeks before use

- Compost tea. Let the water from the tap sit overnight to clear chlorine, which will kill off microbes. Stir in compost material. Use once a week. You can add fish fertilizer and Epsom salts

GROW A VEGETABLE GARDEN IN POTS AND CONTAINERS

Regarding the materials you can use for your DIY composter are concerned, here is a list:

- Leaves; follow the ratios: ⅓ food to ⅔ leaves, grass, and garden clippings

- Coffee grounds and tea filter (make sure to check the tea box to ensure filters are organic)

- Egg shells or any other food scraps Be aware that, when composting meat and dairy, there is a concern for safety because of Salmonella and E. coli since they can transfer to growing plants in the garden

- Christmas trees from your celebrations

- Local state park trail and bring a big bag for browns

- Newspaper, toilet rolls, paper towels, cardboard

- Water from rain barrels or try using the water from the water change in the aquarium (if you have one) since it is rich in nutrients

- Meat, dairy, and anything edible (note: make sure the compost bin is enclosed when composting edibles since it will prevent animals from digging into it)

- Wine bottle natural corks sourced from the "cork oak tree," even though it takes a few years to decompose (note: consider cutting them up after boiling for several minutes or recycling via the paper and plastic recycling method)

- Dead rodents and birds

- If you chop larger pieces of material into smaller pieces, they will decompose more quickly

Larger Size Compost Bin is Better Small Space, Use Small Bin

Another important consideration during building or buying a composting bin is its size. Let me give you some information regarding these so that it is easier for you to decide on one. Since I live in a place that has a somewhat colder climate, I believe a larger size works best for me. Since materials shrink by almost 30 to 40 percent during decomposition, my experience proves that a greater volume provides faster results. However, I recommend you check the size of your yard or any other place you plan on composting first. This way, you can choose a size that will fit perfectly without getting in your way.

This chapter is meant to be enlightening and open doors for gardeners interested in small-space gardening. Overall, I have elaborated on the types of soils that work best for you to be a successful plant parent. You have information on everything from loamy and chalky to silty and sandy. Furthermore, if you remember correctly, I have taught you what you need to look for in the perfect soil. We have gone over all the essential elements as well as their functions. I have elaborated on the process of composting. From DIY compost bins to ready-to-use compost tumblers, you have all you need to know to choose the perfect option. This will allow you to experience the composting process and see how rewarding and miraculous it is. In the upcoming chapter, I will be getting down to business and

GROW A VEGETABLE GARDEN IN POTS AND CONTAINERS

sharing all the techniques regarding the different methods of growing certain vegetables. So, read up, my gardening folks!

Chapter Five

Vegetable Planting and Growth. Seeds and Seedlings

Seeds are Small and Mighty. How does a tiny seed transform into a fruit?

Planting seeds and watching them grow into beautiful and complete plants is awe-inspiring. Imagine a seed just lying dormant, then suddenly it is provided with the condition that helps it thrive. Now, before you know it, it magically transforms into a spectacular plant, be it a fruit, vegetable, flower, or even a tree.

It is truly a wonder and has been one of the many reasons why I love gardening. One of the most intelligent features of plants is that they feed themselves independently. Hence, the term "autotrophs." They self-nourish through photosynthesis by combining the sun's energy and surroundings.

This is what makes plants so undeniably different. I mean, just imagine us humans sitting in the sun and feeding ourselves some soil while breathing in oxygen. Definitely not our cup of tea. We need those complex carbs, fats, and vitamins to ensure our survival. One vitamin deficiency and we are done for.

The growth of a seed, and its transformation into a plant, is essentially what gives us nutrition. For us humans to grow and survive, we need to keep on planting seeds. This is agriculture. Similarly, the idea of developing your yard into a small garden and starting to grow a bunch of seeds is also a step toward agriculture.

So, what does it take to really grow your vegetables? Is it simply to throw some seeds around the soil and sit and wait? Most definitely not!

This may be the starting point since soil and seeds are what you primarily need to grow your vegetables or fruits. But there is more to this process. When I was starting out, I didn't know the ABC of gardening. I was under the impression that all I had to do was dunk some random seeds in the soil and then drown them in a gallon of water.

Over the years, I came to the conclusion that vegetable gardening has a lot of perks. The most convenient feature is that the plants you choose to grow can be grown from seeds with ease.

Planting Your Magic Seeds?

An easy way to do this is to first ensure your soil is damp. If not, then just add some water so that it turns wet.

GROW A VEGETABLE GARDEN IN POTS AND CONTAINERS

Next, fill up your pots or "seed starting trays" with this wet soil. Instead of burying your seed deep into the soil like it's some corpse, just press it firmly onto the top of the soil.

Try to ensure that your pots or trays are covered. For example, use a sheet or a paper towel. This is essential for seed germination since it provides a humid environment.

You'll notice in a few days that the seed has sprouted. This is your cue to remove the covers and set them up in a location where the light is ample. You can water it from time to time or whenever it seems like it needs it.

So, this was seed planting from scratch 101. Pretty simple, right? Just make sure to wash your hands, so you don't end up with the gardener's fingers. You know, with soil nails and stained palms. Or just wear gloves.

I have mentioned "seed starting trays" above. Most of you might not know what these are. These trays are flat trays and have holes in them.

Each hole is supposed to be filled with a small amount of soil and then later a seed. Just under this tray comes another one. This one is called a drip tray. It collects the tiny drips coming from the seed tray. These could be either water or soil.

As far as the humidity dome is concerned, you can get sheets from your local gardening shop or from where you purchased your trays and seeds. These are made from a transparent material that allows you to monitor the seeds instead of constantly having to lift the covers. Lifting the covers will provide aeration and decrease the humidity inside the covers.

Since seed starting is generally done indoors, especially when the weather outside is much colder, you need to get some grow lights. These lights are usually LED and range from fluorescent tubes to T5 tubes to panel lights (Bertelsen, 2020, 1).

When buying seeds, you should always make it a habit to read the packaging. This way, you can read the expiration date. Yes, seeds have expiration dates too. For example, seeds for peppers and corn only have a shelf life of about 2 years. Meanwhile, lettuce and cucumber seeds can stay up to 6 years. Similarly, the seeds of carrots and tomatoes can last approximately 4 years.

GROW A VEGETABLE GARDEN IN POTS AND CONTAINERS

You can store your seeds in a drawer or a section in your fridge. This will ensure that your seeds last you for as long as possible.

Many of you might wonder why it is better to start your seeds indoors, especially when you have ample space and sunlight outside. Let me explain the reasoning by giving you an example to better understand me.

For example, you want to grow tomatoes or eggplants. Generally, these vegetables have a pretty long growing season. Thus, most gardeners, like myself, prefer to start their seeds indoors. This results in the healthy growth of the plant.

Indoor seed starting has many benefits except the ones listed above. Firstly, they are less expensive than buying seedling plants or transplants. This makes it cost-effective, which is a huge plus, especially if you are on a budget. In addition to this, starting a seed by yourself will eventually pay off as a rather productive harvest season.

Here are some vegetables that work best and are convenient to grow by starting your own seed:

Beets: the seeds of a beet usually come as a knob of seeds clumped together. For example, if you plant one seed, you will get 3-4 plants as a result

Peas: since peas are winter vegetables, their seeds can be planted directly around April. However, it is recommended to start the seeds inside in order to help the germination process. Starting them inside also protects them from being animal meals. Yes, you squirrel. I'm talking about you

Squash: this plant is pretty uncomplicated; you can start the seeds for either the winter or summer squash, depending on the season

Tomatoes: this vegetable is not only a garden must-have but is also one of the easiest to grow; start the seed inside and reap its juicy beauty outside

Herbs: these are the most ideal indoor plants, and you can start the seeds with your favorite aromatic ones like oregano, basil, mint, parsley, rosemary, thyme, etc.

Kale: you can also be smug about your organic homegrown kale and make extravagant salads. Just start the seed inside and enjoy. My personal favorite is Lacinato kale; rich in nutrients and absolutely delicious.

Vegetables & Seasons: Hot or Cold?

Many people ignore the fact that a seed is a culmination of the climatic condition it has been provided with. These include temperature, rainfall, sunlight, etc. Give it optimal conditions, and it will thrive. Lack of warmth or freezing temperatures will kill it. All in all, planting your vegetables when the time is right will not only contribute to vigorous and healthy growth but also yield a successful harvest.

All you need to know is that most vegetables belong to either of the two groups: cold-season crops and hot-season crops.

Thus, this requires these particular vegetables to be planted in a season they can bear. For example, a cold-season vegetable plant will grow best if planted at the start of the spring or at the end of autumn since the weather is chilly as winters are nearing.

Cool Season Crops

Essentially, cool-season vegetables can be planted during two seasons. For example, this could be in early summer or late autumn. The key is ensuring they mature when the weather is cooler. This way, these crops are safe from the warmth of the summer season.

Cool Season Temperatures

The temperature required for planting these veggies ranges from 40 to 75°F (4.5 to 24°C). This is the minimum to maximum scale. The ideal range is from 70 to 76°F (21 to 24.5°C) when the temperature is relatively high. However, these plants stop growing if the temperature reaches or crosses 79°F/26°C.

Hardy & Half-Hardy Vegetables

Hardy and half-hardy vegetables can get away with any frost from the winter season and can withstand freezing temperatures. The terms hardy and half-hardy depend on the plant's tolerance level. Basically, you may choose to plant any hardy vegetables after a gap of at least 2 to 4 weeks between the last frost. This explains the fact that the seeds of hardy plants can germinate even when the soil is cold. Plus, the seedlings of these vegetables can endure freezing temperatures. The following is a list of some hardy vegetables that you can grow, especially if you live in a country where you experience cold weather all year around:

"Asparagus | Broccoli | Brussels Sprout | Cabbage | Collard | Garlic | Horseradish | Kale | Kohlrabi | Leek | Onion | Parsley | Pea | Radish | Rhubarb | Rutabaga | Spinach | Turnip" (Albert, n.d.).

On the other hand, the plants that can withstand freezes and frosts for a short time are called half-hardy vegetables, definitely not as long as the hardy ones. They need to be planted at the end of spring. If you plant them too early on, the probability of them not surviving the cold temperatures is too high.

Here is a list of some half-hardy vegetables:

"Beet | Carrot | Cauliflower | Celery | Chard | Chinese Cabbage | Chicory | Globe Artichoke | Endive | Lettuce | Parsnip | Potato | Salsify" (Albert, n.d.).

Warm Season Vegetables

Warm-season vegetables tolerate temperatures ranging from 50°F/10°C (the minimum) to 86°F/30°C (the maximum). They are highly productive when the soil is warm and between 68°F/20°C to 86°F/30°C. Your plants will show at least a minimum growth if they are allowed at least 75°F/24°C. The ideal temperature is between 57°F/14°C and 61°F/16°C.

Tender and Very Tender

Warm seasoned vegetables come under two categories; either tender or very tender. Now, tender vegetables are ideally placed in the soil after two weeks of the last frost, while the very tender ones need three weeks.

Here are some of the tender vegetables:

"New Zealand Spinach | Snap Bean | Sweet Corn | Tomato" (Albert, n.d.).

The following are the very tender ones:

"Cucumber | Eggplant | Lima Bean | Muskmelon | Okra | Pepper | Pumpkin | Squash | Sweet Potato | Watermelon" (Albert, n.d.).

We have already discussed the **perennials** and **annual** vegetables. perennials are plants that can be productive for several years in permanent locations. These could be growing in the ground as well as in raised bed containers.

These are fall and winter annuals:

"Beet | Cabbage | Carrot | Celery | Chinese Cabbage | Collard | Endive | Garlic | Kale | Kohlrabi | Leek | Lettuce | Mustard | Onion | Pea | Swiss Chard" (Gill, 2017).

These are perennials:

"Artichoke | Asparagus | Broccoli | Radicchio | Rhubarb | Spinach | Sweet Potato | Tree Cabbage | Tree Collard | Watercress | Wasabi | Yam" (Huffstetler, 2022)

Regional Planting Calculators

You can always use a regional planting calculator if you are unsure or confused about when to plant. These are sometimes referred to as "seed planting calculators" and are available online. All you have to do is enter your plant and your last frost details, which will provide you with all you need to know. The dates provided are usually an estimate but work pretty well.

Keep Your Plants Healthy (and Happy!)

I have mentioned in the previous chapters that not all plants like to grow side by side with each other. Some plants prefer the company of other plants. So, don't offend your bush beans by planting some tomatoes beside them. Trust me, they're not gonna be happy to share all the sunlight.

As far as incompatible plants are concerned, look out for a few things. Closely follow the size of your plants, the short ones and the tall ones. Plus, think about their requirements as individual plants. How much sunlight do these plants prefer? In the previous example of bush beans next to tomatoes, I highlighted the factor of sunlight. Tomatoes are tall climbing plants prone to provide shade to the very short bush beans next to them. Bush beans like sunlight just as much as the next plant.

Since no one wants a short monotonous garden, here are some tips to avoid plant feuds. All you have to do is to make sure that you plant the tall plants at a good distance from the short ones. This is crucial, especially if your short plants are warm-seasoned and enjoy the sunlight.

Next comes water-loving plants. A hydrophilic and hydrophobic plant will never grow well together. Hence, I would suggest you plant vegetables that have similar nutritional needs. This includes fertilizers as well.

To make it easier, here are some plants that should most definitely not be planted together:

"Asparagus | Bean | Beet | Broccoli | Cabbage | Cucumber | Pea | Soybean | Sunflower | Tomato." (Waterworth, 2021).

Another lesser-known fact and a result of my experience are that black walnuts do not like being in the same room as your staple vegetables like tomatoes, eggplants, and even corn! (Waterworth, 2021).

Other incompatibilities that are quite well known are these combinations:

- "Mint and onions near an asparagus plant

- Pole beans and mustard near some beets

- Anise and dill right next to some carrots

- Cucumber, pumpkin, radish, sunflower, squash, or tomatoes neighboring any potato hills

- Almost all the members of the cabbage family don't like to be close to a strawberry plant

- Cabbage, cauliflower, corn, dill, and potatoes in proximity to tomatoes" (Waterworth, 2021)

Some Plants Crave Companionship

We all need some moral support from time to time. Plants need some companions with them. Of course, they can grow on their own. But who doesn't like a supportive friend?

Similarly, plants can grow near one another and be of help to each other. Companion planting is beneficial and allows you to make use of plants and the healthy relationships they can develop with each other.

First and foremost, most of the companion plants are the ones that are common vegetables that are grown by almost all gardeners in their gardens. The trick? Just move them around and stick to the ones that work best together.

The second advantage is that plants are companions; they stick up for each other and help eliminate pests. This will not only save your plants but save you from the effort of adding pesticides. Who doesn't want a pest-free garden?

So, in a nutshell, the happier the plant, the healthier the crop. Companion planting gets you the most productive harvest and, hence, a better yield.

Here are some plants that can be best friends with each other:

To be used as a reference, not to be memorized!

"**asparagus:** basil, parsley, pot marigold, tomato, beet, bush bean, broccoli, Brussels sprout, cabbage, cauliflower, Chinese cabbage, garlic, kale, kohlrabi, lettuce, onion

GROW A VEGETABLE GARDEN IN POTS AND CONTAINERS

broccoli: beet, celery, cucumber, dill, garlic, hyssop, lettuce, mint, nasturtium, onion, potato, rosemary, sage, spinach, Swiss chard

Brussels sprout: beets, celery, cucumber, dill, garlic, hyssop, lettuce, mint, nasturtium, onion, potato, rosemary, sage, spinach, Swiss chard

bush bean: beet, broccoli, Brussels sprout, cabbage, carrot, cauliflower, celery, Chinese cabbage, corn, cucumber, eggplant, garlic, kale, kohlrabi, pea, potato, radish, strawberry, Swiss chard

cabbage: beet, celery, cucumber, dill, garlic, hyssop, lettuce, mint, nasturtium, onion, potato, rosemary, sage, spinach, Swiss chard

carrot: bean, chive, lettuce, onion, pea, pepper, radish, rosemary, sage, tomato

cauliflower: beet, celery, cucumber, dill, garlic, hyssop, lettuce, mint, nasturtium, onion, potato, rosemary, sage, spinach, Swiss chard

celery: bean, broccoli, Brussels sprout, cabbage, cauliflower, Chinese cabbage, chives, garlic, kale, kohlrabi, nasturtium, tomato

corn: bean, cucumber, melon, parsley, pea, potato, pumpkin, squash, white geranium

cucumber: bean, broccoli, Brussels sprout, cabbage, cauliflower, Chinese cabbage, corn, kale, kohlrabi, marigold, nasturtium, oregano, pea, radish, tansy, tomato

eggplant: bean, marigold, pepper

kale: beet, celery, cucumber, dill, garlic, hyssop, lettuce, mint, nasturtium, onion, potato, rosemary, sage, spinach, Swiss chard

PERCY SARGEANT

kohlrabi: beet, celery, cucumber, dill, garlic, hyssop, lettuce, mint, nasturtium, onion, potato, rosemary, sage, spinach, Swiss chard

lettuce: beet, broccoli, Brussels sprout, cabbage, carrot, cauliflower, Chinese cabbage, chive, garlic, kale, kohlrabi, onion, radish, strawberry

melon: corn, marigold, nasturtium, oregano, pumpkin, radish, squash

onion: beet, broccoli, Brussels sprout, cabbage, chamomile, cauliflower, carrot, Chinese cabbage, kale, kohlrabi, lettuce, pepper, strawberry, summer savory, Swiss chard, tomato

parsley: asparagus, corn, tomato

pea: bean, carrot, chive, corn, cucumber, mint, radish, turnip

pepper: carrot, eggplant, onion, tomato

pole bean: broccoli, Brussels sprout, cabbage, carrot, cauliflower, celery, Chinese cabbage, corn, cucumber, eggplant, garlic, kale, kohlrabi, pea, potato, radish, strawberry, Swiss chard

potato: bean, broccoli, Brussels sprout, cabbage, cauliflower, Chinese cabbage, corn, eggplant, horseradish, kale, kohlrabi, marigold, pea

pumpkin: corn, marigold, melon, nasturtium, oregano, squash

radish: bean, carrot, chervil, cucumber, lettuce, melon, nasturtium, pea

spinach: broccoli, Brussels sprout, cabbage, cauliflower, Chinese cabbage, kale, kohlrabi, strawberry

strawberry: bean, borage, lettuce, onion, spinach, thyme" (Rhoades, 2021).

Stay in Style!
Plant the Most Popular Vegetables

Here are some tips and tricks for growing some of the most popular vegetables in your garden:

BEAN

- The key to growing this all-time favorite veggie is choosing our variety first. Are you a bush bean or a pole bean kind of person? You can select by analyzing the preferences that these plants have. For example, pole beans grow upwards (hence, the name pole) and mostly take up space vertically.

- Bush beans, on the other hand, have a shorter harvest time than pole beans but don't take up a lot of space vertically. Obviously.

- The next step is to plant them, and here are some tips to follow:

- Choose a spot that has a lot of sunlight

- Soil should be warm with a sound drainage system

- Grow in rows with a distance of at least 2 to 3 feet (60-90 centimeters)

TOMATO

- Plant at least 4 to 6 weeks after the last frost

- Place them in sunlight since they need at least 6 hours of direct sunlight

- Get acidic soil with a pH value between 6.2 to 6.8 (drainage should be good)

- Plant different species of tomatoes at a distance. For example, the bush tomatoes should be planted at a distance of 2 feet (60 centimeters) from the staked tomatoes

- Unstaked ones need a distance of no more than 3 to 4 feet (90 to 120 centimeters)

- Plant in rows

CUCUMBER

- Choose between vining and bush cucumbers

- Vining ones grow upwards and have a quick harvest

- Bush ones have a more extended harvest period

- Both can be planted every two weeks

- Cucumbers like humid and warm conditions, so pick a sunny spot for them

- Soil should be fertile with a sound drainage system

- Soil should be slightly on the acidic side (approximately between 6.5 to 7.0)

- Amend and prep the soil by adding compost as well as manure

- Plant seeds in rows and at a distance of 2-3 feet (60-90 centimeters)

GROW A VEGETABLE GARDEN IN POTS AND CONTAINERS

- Always check the instructions on the seed packet before planting the seeds

CARROT

- Plant in loose or sandy soil for the most effortless growth
- Soil should have a sound drainage system
- Plant in either the spring or fall season
- Thin out the seedlings and place them at a distance

HOT PEPPER

- Buy seedlings or start your own seeds
- Start your own seeds by placing 1/4 inch (0.64cm) deep in the soil
- Provide a heat mat for warmth and keep moist
- Plant in a sunny spot
- Water consistently for continuous moisture
- Do not put in too much manure/compost/fertilizer
- Always cut off the first flowers
- Always wear gloves while harvesting

SUMMER SQUASH

- Use a well-composted soil

- Plant at a distance of 3 to 6 feet (90 to 183 centimeters)
- Water only at the soil level

SWEET PEPPER

- Start growing 2 weeks after the last frost
- Choose a sunny spot for the plant to get plenty of sunlight
- Soil should be sandy loam with good drainage
- Use organic material
- Grow at a distance of 2 to 3 feet (60 to 90 centimeters)
- Use bone meal for a healthy growth
- Add mulch to keep the weed away

ONION

- Use acidic soil that drains well
- Start growing in early spring
- Plant in rows at a distance of 6 to 12 inches (15 to 30 centimeters)
- Choose a sunny spot
- Use fertilizer as well

Succession Planting

Succession planting is key to harvesting your vegetables and having a constant source all season long. What exactly is this? Simply put, you must plant your seeds at an interval of 7 to 21 days. This will ensure a constant supply by harvesting your produce throughout the season. These could be the same vegetable or even a different one; your choice! The idea is to start a new crop as soon as you harvest your first one.

Let me give you an example. I, for one, am a radish lover. I consume almost 12 to 14 radishes a week. Now, instead of starting all my radish seeds simultaneously, I will focus on planting the number of seeds that will give me 12 to 14 radishes a week. Similarly, I will plant the same number of seeds in the coming week and the next. This is succession planting.

Determinate and Indeterminate Vegetables

Succession planting is usually done in the care of growing determinate vegetables. Determinate vegetables are crops that produce all of the vegetables at once. On the other hand, indeterminate vegetables are those whose plants will continue to produce vegetables on the same plant. These include tomatoes, cucumbers, peppers, etc.

Keep a Check on Your Vegetables

It's a good idea to use a notebook to keep an update on the plants since it is my go-to move. It is a most helpful step, especially through the growing season. For example, you can record exactly how many tomatoes you harvested from your plant in the last season. Keep a list of it in your notes. Later, use those notes to help you plan for the next season.

For example, you plan on wanting to produce enough food to cater to you throughout the current season and have enough to store for the winter season as well. To do this, if you have noted down the yields of all your plants and kept track throughout, your job will be much easier!

You can do this by tracking the harvest and yields during the growing season and then using that information for the upcoming season. This way, you will feel more confident in your gardening. Plus, it will help you decide whether you want to grow more to consume at the moment or freeze later.

This chapter was all about efficiently growing your vegetables. We introduced the tiny seed as an awe-inspiring phenomenon watching them sprout from the soil, gradually transforming into magnificent plants. We have seen that some types of vegetable seeds are more convenient to grow at home. We have noted the fact that some plants like to cozy up with others, while some want to steer clear of certain other types.

We have learned that different plants favor warm conditions while others prefer colder temperatures, and many only grow at certain times of the year. A regional planting calculator can be useful to help to determine what is best for your needs.

We touched upon the method of succession planting so that your vegetables grow at the same pace but at different times so you can harvest continuously throughout the season.

Next up, we are going to talk about those dreaded garden pests that can cause headaches and frustration. You need to know how to control them

GROW A VEGETABLE GARDEN IN POTS AND CONTAINERS

by keeping an eagle eye open to spot them and eliminate them using certain kinds of effective, non-toxic products.

See you in the next creepy crawly chapter!

Let's Make Failed Beginner Gardening Projects a Thing of the Past!

"The love of gardening is a seed once sown that never dies." ~ Gertrude Jekyll

Remember the sad lettuce story I told you in the introduction? It's my mission to help as many people as possible avoid such an off-putting start to gardening. One gimmicky YouTube video too many, and a would-be-gardener can be discouraged for life.

There are thousands of people out there who love the idea of growing their own food, who long for the flavors, who dream of a reduced grocery store bill, who are desperate to feed their family better... and all it takes is for them to get off on the wrong foot, and that dream is destroyed forever.

I know from my own gardening journey that finding the right information that speaks to you at the level you're at is crucial if you're to see gardening success... and I want to make sure as many people as possible find it. Weekly pasta nights bursting with fresh garden flavors should be within everyone's reach, and I want to make that happen.

But I'm going to need your help.

Without the point of view of gardeners who've tried my methods, this book could be just as gimmicky as one of those dreaded YouTube videos, and as such, it could slip by the eyes of the people who need it the most.

By leaving a review of this book on Amazon, you can stop that from happening. You can show other readers that this is a trusted resource.

GROW A VEGETABLE GARDEN IN POTS AND CONTAINERS

In just a few sentences, you can let other beginner gardeners know how this book helped you and what they can expect to find inside... and that will lead them in the direction of the guidance they're looking for... without a failed lettuce in sight!

Thank you for your help with this. A book is nothing without its readers.

www.amazon.com/review/create-review?&asin=B0BLL1DWDD

Chapter Six

Dealing with Plant Pests

How to Get Rid of Those Insects and Diseases

Every gardener's nightmare begins here. As a plant parent, initially, I would always freak out if I spotted my plant getting attacked by these vile creatures, and it would break my heart. However, over the years, I realized that these are inevitable, and the only option is to prevent or treat them.

Good Bug vs. Bad bug

Bees, for starters, are good bugs. Simply put, a bad bug will eat your plant and stunt its growth. Good bugs, on the other hand, have plenty of benefits. For example, some good bugs help with the pollination process. Pollination is essential for fruits.

GROW A VEGETABLE GARDEN IN POTS AND CONTAINERS

Other good bugs eat weeds. I know, right? what a relief to know that a bug can do your job! Some good bugs even eat the bad ones present in your garden.

Moral of the story: bugs love to eat.

Look Out for Those Pests and Insects

As mentioned before, monitoring and keeping track of your garden is crucial. Pests and insects are inevitable in any garden. The reason for this is the presence of all those delicious and fresh vegetables or fruits that make a sumptuous meal for them. For example, gardens are prone to slugs and pests. Balconies and patios, on the other hand, will experience fewer bugs or slugs.

There are various ways to identify the presence of pests on your plants. You need to keep an eye open for discoloration of the leaves and the general look of the plant. Sometimes your plant might look stunted and not as tall or full as it should. Other times the leaves have holes, or the color is off. Check for signs of fungus around the root or apparent signs of insects.

Here is a list of some common diseases and pests, along with methods to eliminate them:

- *Aphids* - Insects that can infest your plants. They can suck the soul out of them. Spraying them with a strong jet of water is an easy way to get rid of them. Another option is to use an insecticide soap. However, you may need to repeat these steps for permanent removal.

- *Cabbage worms* - A giveaway for the presence of these little fellas is the numerous holes present in your cabbage leaves. The key is to remove any adult and visible worms by hand. Gross, I know, but necessary. Plus, you need to be on the lookout for any eggs hidden under those leaves.

- *Spider mites* – They cause your plant to dry out and die eventually. To get rid of these monsters, try spraying with horticultural soap. It is a tried and tested method.

- *Tomato hornworms* – They are particularly fond of tomato and pepper leaves. These are the "larvae stage" of the infamous five-spotted hawk moth (Iannotti, 2021). These worms camouflage with the garden easily, so it's hard to identify them until the damage is done. However, whether it's in the form of eggs or a fully grown moth, it is not pleasant to the eyes or the garden. Since the size is so large, the only option is to pick them out and get rid of them.

- **_Wireworms_** – These are the most common type of worms present in your soil. They attack the roots causing your plant to grow weak eventually They are so common because it's difficult to remove them. The only option is to cultivate your soil to reveal them as a snack for any birds in the area. You can also stick a piece of sweet potato in your soil. Check for any worms after a couple of days.

- **_Plant viruses_** – If you spot a yellow pattern on your leaves, it is probably an indication of the mosaic virus. The only option is to get rid of the leaves that seem infected to protect the rest of the plant.

- **_Gray mold_** – This common fungus is also called Botrytis. The key is to get rid of any leaves that showcase the fungus. Plus, create plenty of room for healthy airflow. This can be done by cutting any extra foliage in the autumn season.

- **_Powdery mildew_** – Any presence of a powdery residue on the leaves of your plants indicates the growth of this fungus. You can use a fungicide to get rid of this.

Natural Choices to Protect Your Plants

The first instinct upon spotting a bug or pest threatening our harvest is to go in with an insecticide. Fair enough. But who enjoys eating produce that has been treated with toxic chemicals? Let me tell you a little secret: insecticides are available free of harmful chemicals. Yup, you heard that right. All are safe and natural for your organic garden. Some of them are as follows:

- Bacillus thuringiensis - Fancy name, right? This had been a staple among organic farmers and gardeners. It gets rid of all the harmful bugs and pests like worms. However, it doesn't harm any good bugs (remember?) like bees and ladybeetles. Isn't that great? Protect those bees!

- Neem Oil - This is an oil made from the leaves of the neem tree. It is particularly famous in Asia. This has been used for decades as an insecticide. It limits their ability to reproduce as well as feed.

- Spinosad – This is extracted from the Caribbean soil. It is a popular option to control the growth of potato beetles. It kills them quickly.

- Pyrethrin - One of the most effective insecticides since it kills bugs exceptionally quickly.

Pros and Cons of Using Safe Insecticides

The best part about using these safe and neutral insecticides is that they aren't toxic to human beings. Furthermore, they do not thrive in the environment, so they are safe to use. However, the majority of these take a long time to be effective and require repeated doses.

INTEGRATED PEST MANAGEMENT (IPM)

In simple words, integrated pest management, aka IMP, focuses on an environment-friendly approach to pest management. It revolves around practices that stem from common sense. It basically involves securing information about the life cycle of a pest or insect and the kind of interaction or relation it has with the environment. The key is to use this information, alongside the methods available for pest management, to create something that gets the job done while simultaneously protecting the consumers and the environment. The point is to be economical but not hazardous to others.

We also discussed all those disgusting bugs and fungi that can attack our garden and stunt the growth of our plants.

I suggested to you the many methods you may use to eliminate these annoying creatures. We also briefly shed some light on integrated pest management IPM and its meaning.

Previously, we have summarized the seasons and climate and their effects on the plant's growth. We have also discussed some climatic conditions of different countries like Australia and Germany and the kind of plants that grow there.

My upcoming chapter plans to go deep into the idea of growing seasons, world climates, biodiversity, and the different growing regions, including micro-climates. Consider it a simple and fun lesson on climatology. It will help you assess the hours of direct sunlight that shines on some areas around the house and through the windows. This will aid you in understanding how much shade is around the premises of your potential garden. You will also learn to identify the microclimate around where you live. All this will ensure that you make the best use of the conditions to grow the best varieties of vegetables.

Chapter Seven

Understanding Growing Seasons in Different Regions of the World

The primary purpose of this chapter is to understand the climatic conditions of different parts of the world in relation to the kind of vegetables and plants you want to grow. Let us start with climate. What exactly is climate? Simply put, the climate is characterized as the "long-term pattern of weather in a specific region" (Edwards, 2022).

All in all, different parts of the world display different climates. For example, some parts are hot, humid, and rainy, like the tropics. On the other hand, some are cold and dry, like Canada or Alaska. This shows that climates vary broadly from hot to cold depending on where we are, relative to the north and south poles. Climates and their associated temperatures also tend to fluctuate at different altitudes.

Speaking of plants and their growth, it doesn't matter whether you live in the colder northern or southern regions, the Mediterranean regions, desert regions, or tropical regions. The 12 principles of plant biology apply to every plant regarding its growth, regardless of its location or climate.

Twelve Principles of Plant Biology

Some of you might not be familiar with the twelve plant biology principles. Don't worry. I'm here to shed some light on these facts. Before I provide you with the list of principles, I want you to understand why it is a good idea for us to understand these principles and their significance. These principles concerning plant biology provide a framework for us to understand the plants' intricacies and acknowledge how plants create and sustain life.

GROW A VEGETABLE GARDEN IN POTS AND CONTAINERS

The twelve principles are as follows:

1. "The biological mechanisms and biochemistry used by animals, microorganisms, and plants are similar. However, plants' use of chemicals and sunshine to grow makes them uniquely different. The world's supply of food and energy is produced via the process known as photosynthesis.

2. Numerous inorganic components from the soil are necessary for plant growth. In the biosphere, plants are crucial to the movement of these micronutrients.

3. Plants have contributed to the evolution of life, including the atmospheric contribution of oxygen and ozone, by evolving from ocean-dwelling, algae-like progenitors.

4. In flowering plants, sexual reproduction occurs, resulting in a seed's development. Asexual propagation is another method of reproduction.

5. Animals, many microorganisms, and plants all use respiration and energy for growth and reproduction.

6. Cell walls offer the plant structural strength, fibers, and building blocks for people, insects, birds, and many living things.

7. There are about 350,000 species of plants, ranging in size and appearance from tiny cells to enormous trees.

8. Plants are the primary source of fiber, medications, and a vast array of other essential items used daily.

9. Similar to animals, plants are susceptible to harm and demise from infectious diseases brought on by microbes. Unique mechanisms exist for plants to protect themselves from pathogens and pests.

10. The central molecule in plant cells and tissues is water. It is crucial for the structure, development, and movement of salts and organic compounds within plants.

11. Hormones govern the growth and maturation of plants, and they are influenced by environmental pressures, light, gravity, touch, and other external signals.

12. Plants may survive in a range of situations by adapting. In ecosystems, plants offer a variety of homes for birds, pollinating insects, and other creatures" (*The 12 Principles of Plant Biology | American Society of Plant Biologists*, n.d.).

WHAT IS A GROWING SEASON?

You have read this phrase throughout this book. But what do growing seasons mean? A growing season is a time within a year when crops and other plants grow successfully, but the length of a growing season can vary from place to place (Abercrombie, 2022).

As mentioned before, the season and duration vary from plant to plant and vegetable to vegetable. For example, the growing season in Italy could be highly different from Brazil. To put it simply, the growing season of a plant or vegetable is the season where the crop grows the most.

So, what factors affect the growing seasons? Generally speaking, the single most crucial factor in determining a season is the intensity of sun rays it gets or experiences. However, this intensity is never constant. The earth is tilted on its axis by around 23 degrees from the plane of its yearly orbit around the sun. In other words, it is tilted over from the vertical.

Consequently, the sun's rays heat the northern and southern parts of the globe at different times of the year. That is why we get summers and winters.

The climate conditions around the equator remain constant throughout the year because it is not affected by the tilt.

Suppose it's the summer season where you live. This means that your part of the earth is facing the sun and getting those sun rays, increasing the temperature. It's that simple, right?

Growing Seasons Around the globe

For example, in the state of Alaska, the growing season's duration is only about 105 days approximately. However, during the growing season, there are 24 hours of sunlight.

PERCY SARGEANT

Can you imagine? The reason for this is that the arctic is tilted towards the sun. This causes several vegetables, like cabbages, to grow into huge sizes. And trust me when I say this, huge! These weigh about 75 lbs each. Imagine the size!

Now let us move on down to the tropics. The warm climate in the tropics is probably responsible for this area's growing season lasts almost the entire year. The only obstacle in the growing season is when it rains. Obviously, most crops don't do too well during the rainy seasons. Coffee usually grows in a tropical climate.

Brazil, for instance, is a tropical country and one of the largest producers of coffee. However, it has a fluctuating growing season in Brazil due to the disruption from the rain. Indonesia gets its fair share of rain, which usually disrupts the coffee's growing season. On the other hand, since Colombia isn't too wet and experiences less rainfall, the growing season lasts all year around.

In other tropical areas that don't get ample rainfall and are considered too dry, growing seasons are almost non-existent. An example of this would include the region of the Sahel in north Africa. This area is located at the midpoint of the Savanna and the Sahara Desert. Hence, the site is too dry and experiences droughts as well. These are the regions that experience dramatic weather patterns.

Let us look at the more temperate countries. These include states in Europe as well as America. The temperate areas enjoy the typical weather, that is, warm summers and cool winters. Both kinds of weather are enjoyable and tolerable. The growing seasons in these regions are relatively long and can last up to 8 months.

To put it simply, the region's distance from the equator affects the growing season's length. The further it is from the equator, the shorter the growing season. Similarly, the closer it is to the equator, the longer the growing seasons will be. For example, we have talked about the European countries and the states in America experiencing longer growing seasons.

However, the growing season gets shorter as we move further from the equator and closer to the poles. For example, as mentioned before, Alaska, located around the north pole, only has a growing season of about 105 days. This is approximately 3 months compared to the 8 months experienced in the rest of America. Crazy, right?

What's the Growing Season in your Neck of the Woods?

It must seem daunting not knowing what the growing season is in your area. However, it is easy to determine your own. Most small space gardeners are usually based in temperate regions. There are two ways in which you can measure the growing season. It all depends on the first and last frost that your area experiences. All you have to do is, calculate the average number of days between this period, that is, the first extreme frost in autumn and the last frost in spring (Abercrombie, 2022). This is the first option.

The second option is to observe and calculate the average number of days where the temperature is high enough to trigger your plant to either sprout or grow (Abercrombie, 2022).

However, this calculation varies from plant to plant. For example, tomatoes thrive the most, between 50 to 80°F (10 to 27°C). Similarly, since spinach is a cool-weather leafy green vegetable, the optimum temperature for its growth is between 50 to 60°F (10 to 16°C).

Most plants will not be able to tolerate the frost that comes during the autumn season and might die before growing fully. So, plant your vegetables in their optimum growing season. This means you should plant after the last frost of the spring season. Especially if you live somewhere that has a shorter growing season. If you choose to plant too late in a short growing season, the plants will not make it to maturity.

Know Your Zone!

What is a plant hardiness zone? Big words, I know. In easy terms, a hardiness map is constructed to give gardeners an idea of what plants and vegetables have the probability of thriving in a particular location or area. One of the most renowned maps is the USDA Plant Hardiness Zone Map made by the United States Department of agriculture. Another one is known as Natural Resources Canada (NRC).

Since most of you are first-time gardeners, the idea of these hardiness zones might intimidate and confuse you. They look so complicated. I was thrown off the first time I saw it. However, I discovered later on the benefits of these zones. You will be able to plant the vegetables that can grow and thrive where you live. This will allow you to grow them year after year successfully.

Please note that these planting zones are just suggestions and estimates.

Not all plants can survive every climate condition. Some can tolerate extreme temperatures, while some can die when temperatures rise.

For those living in an area that experiences microclimates, please remember that these planting zones are just suggestions and estimates. Don't see them as strict zones with instructions to follow. Consider them a guide.

This is the USDA Plant Hardiness Zone Map:

https://melnor.com/usda-hardiness-zone-map/

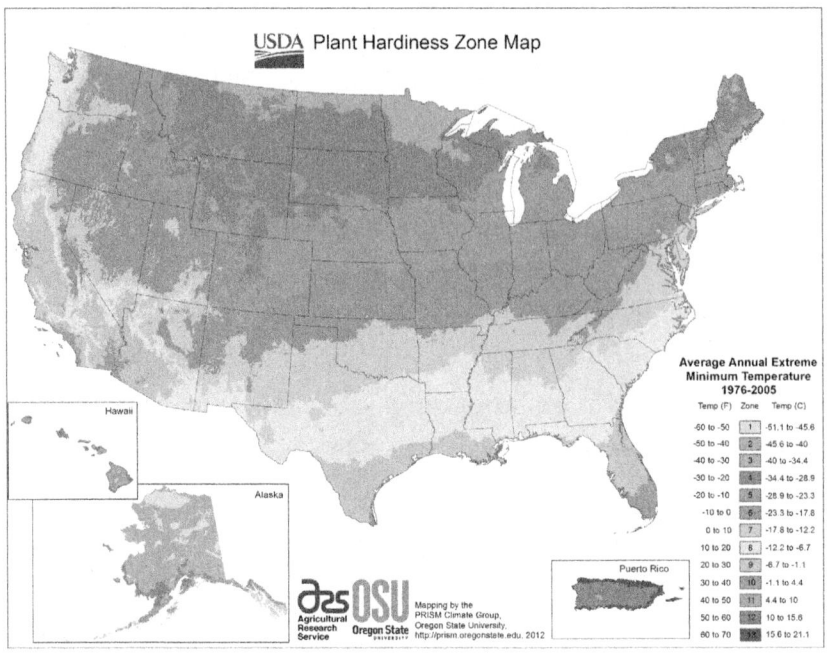

This is how the map breaks down:

"the map shows the average annual minimum winter temperatures of each region and is divided into thirteen distinct 10ºF/-12°C zones, which are further divided into sub-zones of 5°F/-15°C " (*What's Your Planting Zone? | USDA Plant Hardiness Zone Map*, 2022).

If you live in the United States, the seed packets you buy usually have their hardiness zone written on the back. This is generally indicated as a number. The map from the USDA is color-coded for your convenience. It makes it easy to comprehend as well.

You can understand and use the planting zones in different ways. These are especially useful for those of you who want to grow perennials. As discussed earlier, perennials are vegetables that continue to produce fruit without you having to plant them again and again. This requires perennials to withstand the winter season. It implies that you must plant perennials such as shrubs and trees in the correct planting zone. A sure shot is to plant native species. These are the ones that grow naturally in the environment.

Let me be considerate and acknowledge the people not living in the United States. People in Canada also have their zone maps. But what of the rest? There is nothing to worry about. This is because several websites allow you to recognize the planting zones in your area and country. The US, UK, and Canada have zone maps that are quite easy to comprehend. These maps use minimum and maximum temperatures endured by plants to indicate their planting zones.

You can simply convert the hardiness zones to calculate your own specific zone.

And then there is the Australian Plant Hardiness Zone Map:
https;//www.diggers.com.au/pages/climate-maps-for-plants

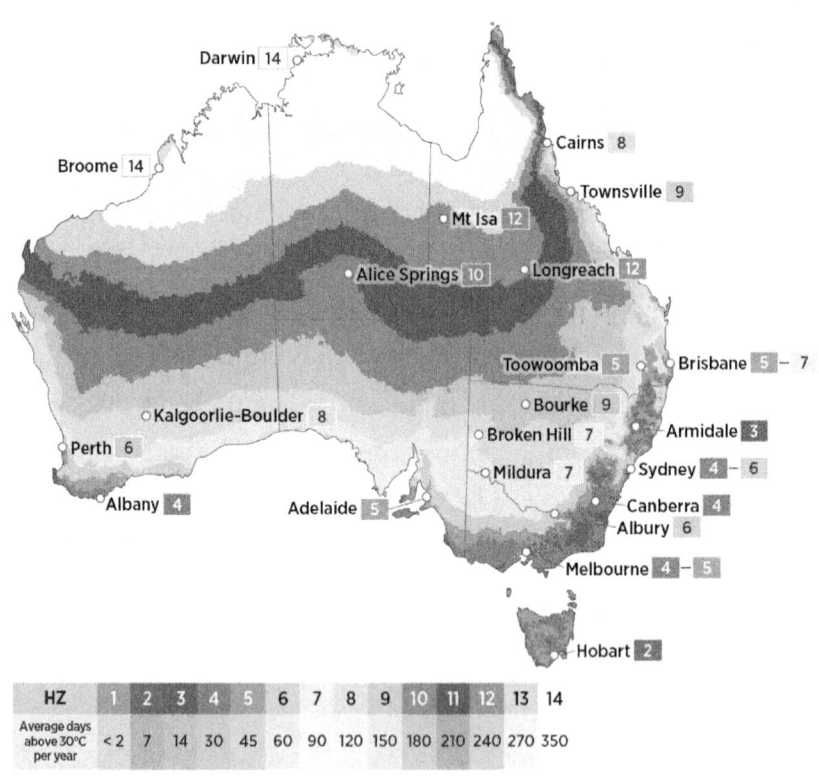

For example, suppose you live in Australia. In that case, all you have to do is: "measure the average lowest temperature of your region and add ten degrees for each higher zone. The US zone 11 has an average lowest temperature of 40°F/4.4°C. Similarly, for zones with higher low temps, such as zone 13, the average lowest temperature would be 60°F /15°C)" (Grant & Cathey, 2021).

The European Plant Hardiness Zone Map:

https://vividmaps.com/hardiness-zones-of-europe/

However, you only need to do this method if your country doesn't have a zone map. Most countries like Australia, New Zealand, Africa, Canada, China, Japan, Europe, Russia, and South America have their own systems for the hardiness zone maps. So even if your country doesn't have one, it shouldn't be a problem!

MICROCLIMATES: SUNLIGHT AND SHADE

So far, we know what climate is, but what is a microclimate? As the name suggests, it is basically the smaller climates that exist in the area we live in. As usual, this climate is also a culmination of several factors, including rainfall, sunlight, wind, and temperature.

Even inside your home, there is a microclimate.

Most homes have at least four distinct microclimates, with one on each side. One can have its front facing north, south, east, or west. A home frequently has many orientations, such as northwest and southeast. Certain home styles may have more based on the modifications to the basic four-sided construction.

Many people are apprehensive about growing vegetables and fruits simply because they're not sure they have adequate sunlight. I was one of them. Obviously, 8 hours of direct sun isn't a luxury everyone has. Let me bust this little myth once and for all. Yes, it is problematic, but contrary to popular belief, it isn't impossible altogether.

Here are a few tips for those of you who don't get much direct sun:

- Firstly, check the level and hours of sunlight you get. For example, morning and afternoon sun are highly different in terms of temperature. If you have hot afternoons, even with just 4 to 5 hours of sunlight, it is more than enough for you to grow your vegetables

- Choose flowering vegetables if you get good hot sun. These include tomatoes, peas, and cucumbers. Of course, you could grow them in less sun, but it won't yield the same taste.

- If you don't get enough sun, some vegetables can tolerate shade: leafy green vegetables like lettuce, kale, or spinach. Widely speaking, most leafy vegetables have a shade tolerance

As they say, "If you grow it for the fruit, it needs full sun. The partial sun is all you need if you grow it for the leaves."

GROW A VEGETABLE GARDEN IN POTS AND CONTAINERS

This chapter has majorly emphasized the importance of climate and all the factors that contribute to it. These include temperature, rainfall, wind as well as sunlight. You have also learned that the kind of plants you want to grow and the kind of plants you can grow are directly dependent on your climate type.

More than that, the kind of microclimate you experience inside your home. All in all, this was a simple lesson on the basics of climatology and plant growing. Now that we have learned the basics of planting vegetables, it is time to know what to do once your veggies grow, that is, how to harvest them.

So, don't leaf just yet - keep on reading! (Yes, the pun was intended.) This is precisely what the next chapter has in store for you.

Chapter Eight

Harvesting and Preserving Vegetables

It is known among most gardeners that the more one gardens, the more there is to learn. Let us be honest, why do people even bother to grow vegetables? There's plenty of stock available in the grocery store. Yes, even organic. The answer is simple: the quality and taste of the veggies you harvest and bring to the table are a class apart.

Harvesting vegetables at the right time is precisely what makes commercial store-bought vegetables so different from homegrown ones. The commercial ones are harvested early since they need to store these vegetables. Hence, it is best for them to harvest before these vegetables are ready. This is precisely what makes home gardening and homegrown produce so much better! At home, you can reap the moment your vegetable reaches its peak to enjoy it to the maximum.

Squishy & Overripe Vegetables? No, Thank You.

Harvesting vegetables is not a pesky task. Once you get the hang of a few basic dos and don'ts, you're good to go!

Here are some basic tips for newbie gardeners:

The key is to pick your veggies with care. Since the fruit is ripe, it can be easily bruised. So, be gentle. Keep a firm grip but avoid being too hard.

It is essential to snap off your vegetables with a nice clean cut. There are certain vegetables that have stems that have a natural "breaking point" (Miller, 2021). Others, however, will only break once you physically remove the fruit. To ensure that you don't damage the plant and halt any yield, it is vital to use a scissor, knife, or any other sharp object to remove the fruit with a clean cut.

The next step (literally) is to step with the utmost care. Think of walking on eggshells. Not really, but why not? If it means you'll be careful. Walking casually around your garden puts plants at high risk for damage. You can easily step on any vines. This can not only put the plant in grave danger but could also be a starting point for any disease.

Whenever harvesting, use a basket. Baskets that are low and have a horizontal design can save your fruits and vegetables from getting damaged. How? Well, it is simple. A long tall container will create a weight that will push down on those poor veggies causing them to get squished and bruised. Who wants a squished rotten tomato? Trust me, you will thank me later. I know I don't.

Last but not least is to not ignore your plants. No, they do not deserve silent treatment. This is crucial if you live somewhere that is warm, sunny, and gets plenty of rainfall. All these factors can help your plant mature quickly. So, it is critical to keep checking out these fellas.

It is About Time. But When?

Harvesting is easy, yes, but that doesn't mean that you take it too lightly. There are rules that you can follow if you want an easier life. For starters, harvest on time. They say the early bird catches the worm. Well, in this case, fruit. Or vegetables.

Vegetables are best harvested early in the morning. Period. Why not let them spend the night in the garden? Here's why: "overnight vegetables tend to regain the moisture they lost during the sunny day. This allows the starches or carbs formed during the day to turn into sugars" (Tanner & Ballew, 2020).

In simple words, early morning veggies will be crisper, juicier, and much sweeter. Overnight harvested ones? Well, the opposite of all these. Now, we don't want that, right?

Some gardeners like to follow the rule "the bigger, the better." In the case of plants, this is probably not always the best approach. For example, numerous gardeners think leaving the okra pods on the plant for a longer time will yield a better harvest. Wrong. So wrong.

Leaving them too long can cause them to be over-mature and over-woody. Result? Inedible okras.

For some reason, if some of you cannot harvest early in the morning, I suggest keeping your vegetables out of sunlight. This allows them to cool slowly and also slow down the degeneration process. Just remember this one thing: whenever the harvest nears, collect at that time since it results in the best produce. The later, the worse.

Principles of Harvesting

For maximum taste and nutrients: beans, peas, summer squash, and turnips, among other vegetables, are at their tastiest and healthiest when they are young and soft. For other vegetables to have fully formed tastes, such as tomatoes, melons, and winter squash, they must be allowed to be fully mature on the vine.

Harvest based on size: although size is typically a trustworthy predictor of maturity, it sometimes requires some knowledge to determine whether a vegetable is genuinely ready for plucking. Always examine seed packages or any material that is supplied with purchased transplants for recommendations on mature vegetable sizes since there could be some variation in vegetable kinds.

Harvest regularly: overlooking to harvest veggies routinely is one of the worst errors a gardener can make. Unpicked beans can quickly go from being tender to becoming harsh. A few days ago, a zucchini that was just 2 inches long may now be an overripe 2-foot long club. Remember that the plant's objective is to reproduce. Vegetable plants will stop producing if they are allowed to reach full maturity and are not picked.

Harvest with the proper equipment: some plants, like lettuce, kale, and peas, must be carefully snipped off with your fingers or plucked. Cut off any vegetables that are difficult to remove from the plant. A specialized set of scissors is appropriate for certain plants, like beans. Harvesting vegetables with more rigid stems, like cucumbers and eggplants, calls for the use of a sharp knife or hand pruners. Harvesting potatoes and other root vegetables are best done using a garden fork.

Harvest in ideal circumstances: At the point of harvest, vegetable quality is at its peak; after that, it starts to decline quickly. The early morning when the dew has dried, is the optimum time of day to pick the majority of veggies. They are at their tastiest and juiciest during this time. Avoid harvesting veggies in the heat of the day since they might quickly wilt, particularly leafy ones.

Handle plants gently. Maintain correct trellising for vining plants to prevent the plant stems from bending or breaking under the weight of growing veggies. A vegetable should not be pulled or torn off the plant. As a result, pathogens may enter the plant and cause harm. Additionally, avoid going around veggies while it's rainy to prevent accidentally spreading fungus and other illnesses to nearby plants.

From the core of the plant, lettuces and other green crops grow. Leafy vegetables should initially be harvested from the outer (bigger) leaves. Pick the bigger outer leaves first, and leave the little new growth in the middle to continue growing (Chadwick, 2020).

Let us talk about some of the more popular vegetables and their harvesting process!

TOMATO – Fruit should be chosen when wholly developed on the vine but still hard; the majority are dark red, although different hues are available according to the type. The shade should be provided for tomatoes after harvest. When picking immature (green) fruit, don't put it in the refrigerator because doing so prevents ripening. Ripen them at 70°F/21°C instead. Green tomatoes may ripen without any light. For one to three weeks, green tomatoes can be kept at a temperature of 50 to 70 °F (10 to 21°C). For 4 to 7 days, ripe tomatoes can be held in the refrigerator or at room temperature (70°F/21°C). Refrigeration, however, has the potential to mute the flavor and give tomatoes a gluey consistency (Tanner & Ballew, 2020)

GROW A VEGETABLE GARDEN IN POTS AND CONTAINERS

BEAN – Just before seeds expand, harvest the beans when they are full-sized. In the refrigerator, beans may be kept for about a week (Miller, 2021)

LETTUCE – Pick the outer leaves when they are at a size that is suitable for harvesting. A single harvest may be made by pulling the entire head. When kept in the crisper drawer of the refrigerator in a zipped bag, lettuce may last for approximately two weeks (Miller, 2021)

ONION – Once the onion tops start to yellow and fall over, dig them up. Cured onions should be stored for a long time at room temperature. Onions that have been appropriately cured can be kept for about 4 months in a warm, dry environment (Miller, 2021)

PEPPER – When green bell peppers are the size of a softball, start picking them. The peppers can also be left on the plant to develop their mature color. They may be kept in the refrigerator for around two weeks (Miller, 2021)

Preserve and Store!

A surplus of vegetables is often something that a gardener experiences. Yes, you may give away those extra fruits or vegetables to your friends and family. But did you know that you could still keep all that organic produce for yourself?

Here's how to preserve your vegetables:

FREEZE – One of the simplest and most efficient ways to preserve food. Invest in a vacuum sealer for the most outstanding results; the secret to successful freezing is ensuring that as little air enters your storage. Doing this may prevent your food's freezer burn and flavor loss. Foods that have recently been prepared should be completely cool before being added. Heat may defrost goods already in your freezer by lowering their temperature, producing steam, which speeds up freezer burn (Lee, 2020).

CAN – Canning is one of the more difficult techniques for preserving veggies. Still, the procedure is easy if you take the time and follow the guidelines properly. Canning must be done carefully because if some items aren't handled properly, hazardous germs may grow on them. Most fruits and certain vegetables may be canned in a boiling water bath. Still, a pressure canner must be used to process low-acid vegetables like squash, peas, beans, carrots, and maize (Dyer, 2022). Canning may also be done using sand. Why? Sand controls humidity, preventing extra liquid from getting near the vegetable to cause rot and increasing the product's lifespan. Root vegetables like carrots and beets are a great choice! (Grant, 2022).

DRY – Vegetables may be dried using a variety of methods, and they are simple to rehydrate for use in soups and casseroles. The simplest way is using an electric food dryer. And you can also dry vegetables in an oven or in direct sunlight. Some fruits and vegetables, like peppers, can be strung on a thread and dried in a cool, well-ventilated space (Dyer, 2022).

PICKLE – The veggies are covered in a boiling brine made of vinegar, salt, and pepper (or sugar for a sweet brine). The jars are tightly sealed when the brine has cooled. It should be noted that while certain pickled veggies may be kept in the fridge for up to a month, others must be canned if you don't want to consume them right away.

If you prefer to **pickle veggies**, place them in a glass canning jar with your desired seasonings, such as:

Dill | Celery Seed | Mustard Seed | Cumin | Oregano | Turmeric | Jalapeno Pepper

Here is a list of vegetables that are a popular option for pickling:

Cucumber | Beet | Carrot | Cabbage | Asparagus | Bean | Pepper | Tomato

Preserving in oil? Follow these rules:

- Cooking veggies is required. They can be roasted, grilled, or blanched

- If you plan to preserve something for more than a week, choose clean, sterile jars

- Two parts of olive oil and one part of vinegar make up the marinade. Also, add salt and pepper. Harmful germs will be kept at bay by the acid and salt

- As long as the vegetables are thoroughly covered in the marinade liquid, and there are no raw ingredients present, the marinated vegetables, when refrigerated, will keep for three to four months (like raw garlic or herbs - I remove these if storing for longer than a week).

- In the refrigerator, the olive oil will solidify; this is a positive indication. Your refrigerator is not cool enough if the oil does not solidify after 24 hours. Freezer? Yes! (Fountaine, 2016).

Use Natural Ingredients

Are you aware that natural ingredients are probably present in your pantry right now that can be used for preservation?

See for yourself:

- ***GARLIC:*** antibacterial & antiviral

- ***HIMALAYAN SEA SALT:*** the best natural preservative

- ***SPICY INGREDIENTS:*** fight bacteria, natural preservation qualities (example: cayenne & mustard)

- ***LEMON:*** a natural source of citric acid, helps prevent spoiling

- ***SUGAR:*** triggers osmosis and aids food to get rid of excess moisture plus other microorganisms

Crazy, right? These simple ingredients have so much more to them than just flavor.

You've Been Served (Not Literally)

Preserved fruits and vegetables are simply delicious. They elevate every dish. They, of course, can be consumed on their own.

Here are some ideas for you about serving and presenting them:

- add to cheese plates
- add to charcuterie boards
- add to mezze platters
- toss into salads
- toss into pasta or grain salads
- add to sandwiches

This chapter has been pretty fun, right? I feel like we've learned so much! The most important and maybe the most rewarding part about gardening is harvesting the fruits of your efforts (in this case, of course, vegetables). Plus, I also told you guys all the fun and creative ways in which you may be able to store those extra veggies. For all of you who have come this far, I'm so happy for you all!

We're moving toward the end of the book, and I have something interesting for you all: the greenhouse! We'll, be doing greenhouse 101, from the basics to the benefits. So, what are you waiting for? Keep reading, gardeners one and all!

Chapter Nine

The Wonders of a Greenhouse

We've all heard the term greenhouse, right? Most of us associate it with greenhouse gasses or effects. But do you know what a greenhouse actually is? Simply speaking, a greenhouse is meant to be a temporary or permanent structure covered in a translucent material that filters sunlight which warms the structure and its interior.

Most experienced gardeners love the idea of a greenhouse. They tend to believe that it is the bee's knees. They are aware of the various benefits of having a greenhouse. On the other hand, most newbies aren't quite aware of what makes a greenhouse so beneficial. Well, no need to fret. I'm here to explain the advantages of keeping a greenhouse in some detail.

Greenhouse Benefits

The first great thing about keeping a greenhouse is that you can control the environment of the plants. You decide everything! From the light and temperature to the soil and moisture. You are in control!

A greenhouse is meant to be a safe haven for your plants. It acts as a protection for all your plants. From insects and bugs to other harmful creatures, a greenhouse shields the inside world from the outside. It also helps if you live in harsh weather conditions since the greenhouse reduces any exposure.

Plants grown in a greenhouse tend to be much healthier than the rest plants on the outside. This is due to the controlled environments and limited exposure to outside conditions. Since the plants are growing in optimal conditions, their growth reflects the protective surroundings.

Decide on Your Perfect Greenhouse

We now know the benefits of keeping a greenhouse. Setting up a greenhouse is an entirely different process. There are so many choices available in the market when it comes to greenhouse kits. A lot of variations are present in terms of size, design, and prices. It can be a little intimidating, for sure, but don't be concerned. Let us discuss some basics about deciding on the perfect greenhouse for you. The first thing to consider is the size of the greenhouse. If you're struggling from the price point of view and just want a place to start your seeds, a lovely small starter greenhouse is the right option for you. By adding in a potting bench alongside some soil and seeds, you're good to go!

GROW A VEGETABLE GARDEN IN POTS AND CONTAINERS

Similarly, if you're someone who is an avid believer in "go big or go home," a grower setup is what you can go for. This will have more room for your plants to grow and expand.

My advice is that it's best to utilize as much space as possible when considering buying a greenhouse kit for yourself. You could get one large greenhouse that fits the entire available space or two smaller ones for the same space. Your choice!

Glazing Options

Three glazing options are available for your greenhouse panels: opaque (diffused), clear and semi-diffused. If your main aim is to just start the seeds and transplant them outside, it is better to go for clear glass panels since the seedlings require ample direct sunlight. Another option for clear ones is to use polycarbonate.

However, if you plan to grow your plants until their maturity, the direct sun might not be the best option, so it's better to diffuse it. Multi-walled polycarbonate and twin-walled polyethylene both provide well-diffused light. This will allow the plants to carry on with photosynthesis and grow. If you want the light to be there but be just a little diffused, semi-diffused is for you.

Insulation From the Cold

Insulation is key if you're living in a place where you experience harsh winters. Multiple-walled polycarbonate is a good choice. Another option is to go for twin-walled polyethylene. It gives a soft, diffused light and impeccable insulation with much more flexibility than hard polycarbonate (Seaman, 2022).

Simple tempered glass panels or single-walled polycarbonate do the job for milder winters. A cheaper option is polythene film which is used quite often.

A greenhouse can be done in any way and designed to fit your aesthetic. You can get an appropriate kit and start by undertaking all the factors.

How about an Indoor Greenhouse?

Ever wondered what the purpose of an indoor greenhouse is? Well, many people aren't blessed with ample outdoor space they can set up for gardening. A greenhouse is ideal for people living in apartment buildings.

Look around your house and use your imagination. You don't need a vast room. You'll undoubtedly be able to fit your indoor gardening equipment in a corner. You may guarantee the garden receives adequate sunshine by positioning it, for instance, in the corner of the kitchen counter, on your living room table, or on a windowsill. Indoor greenhouses are also a great way to enhance the beauty of your home. Plus, they are easy to move, making them a portable garden! Here are some benefits:

- Since they are smaller than your conventional ones, they are easy to move

- A greenhouse also protects your plants from harsh weather outside, whether wind or storm. A greenhouse is easy to control because you have control over everything, from the temperature to the humidity. So you can regulate everything accordingly. Grow lights do the trick if you don't have enough sunlight. It's better to keep a combination; of sunlight and artificial lights

- Also, suppose the temperature isn't warm enough. In that case, you might require a heater and a thermometer to keep the temperature in check

- In addition, if you plan on leaving the greenhouse for several days, you might want to invest in a water irrigation system. Depending on the type, it can cost around 25 US dollars or more

Choose The Perfect Spot

The best location for your greenhouse is where it will get ample sunlight. Near a window is a great option. A patio will also do. Plus, the spot should be warm and humid. Once you decide on the size, the place will be easy to choose.

What to grow indoors?

People who garden indoors mostly prefer to grow herbs. They are fast to grow and do not require extensive care.

Here are several herbs suggestions that you can grow:

"Basil | Chive | Mint | Oregano | Parsley | Rosemary | Thyme" (Guide & Gemeš, 2021).

If you plan on growing vegetables, you may start with the following:

"Carrot | Cucumber | Hot Pepper | Lettuce | Radish | Spinach | Tomato" (Guide & Gemeš, 2021).

Note: A great mini greenhouse with 4 shelves costs between $60 and $90 US with 8 shelves. A walk-in will set you back about $90 US. (these were the prices at the time of writing this book) You can visit a store or just check out on Amazon and Target! The designs and options are endless.

Try an Outdoor Greenhouse

We know all the basics of an indoor greenhouse, right? Let's move out now. Here are some factors that you might want to consider.

Like everything else in life, a greenhouse can be as small or as big as you want. It just depends on the size of the space you have. In addition, it is also essential to think of what you plan to plant in your greenhouse.

For example, a little greenhouse might suffice if you just want to start your seedlings. Similarly, suppose the plan is to fully grow the vegetables. In that case, getting a bigger one where the plants can mature and expand is better.

Deciding on the size is essential because expanding once you've built yourself a greenhouse is challenging.

Yes, There are Greenhouse Kits

Most gardeners like to buy kits for their greenhouses. These are especially useful if trying to make your greenhouse from scratch. It makes the process much more convenient. There are a lot of options available for affordable and well-made kits.

These kits are made up of different materials. Here are some options:

- It's not advisable to go for a wooden kit since it will trap the humidity and allow the wood to degrade

- A more durable option is to use a plastic PVC made of tubes. However, constant sun exposure might risk it becoming brittle

- The most durable out of all is probably the metal kits

- Aluminum is an affordable option

- Steel ones are much more expensive and hard to find

- Twin and triple polycarbonates are readily available

- Glass is not recommended

You can find all these kits on Target and Amazon. Plus, you could also visit a nearby gardening store which might have a few options for you.

Walk-In Greenhouse

As the name suggests, these greenhouses are where you can directly walk in and take care of your plants. There is a lot of headroom in these greenhouses, making them quite tall. Most are equipped with shelves to allow room for the gardener to stand and inspect.

Climbing plants and tall shrubs are excellent plants for a walk-in greenhouse due to the available vertical space.

Owning a greenhouse is beneficial if you suffer from an aching back since you won't have to bend as much. Thus, a solution to backbreaking gardening!

Lighting

Outdoor greenhouses don't require artificial lighting. This is because they absorb plenty of UV light from the sun's rays. However, if you are planting a couple of plants that are shade-loving, the shade would be lovely! A rolled-up sheet of polypropylene, screens of wood or aluminum, vinyl plastic shading, or paint-on materials can all be used as a shade for your plants (Vinje, 2012).

Nutrients

Some gardeners are under the impression that greenhouse plants require additional nutrients or care. That is not true. Just like any other plant in a conventional garden, a greenhouse plant also requires basic essential nutrients like a good potting mix of soil and fertilizer. For greenhouse plants, you may start fertilizing them twice a week. Follow these guidelines for best results.

Ventilation

Ventilation is crucial. You may physically open the vents. However, it is most important to monitor the temperature. This is because even in winter, the plants can get too warm. You may like to invest in automatic hydraulic vents, which are electric and temperature sensitive. Or, you could get a basic oscillating fan to keep the air moving. Ventilation will prevent any diseases and maintain the health of your plants.

Supplies

Greenhouse gardening requires some supplies. The following are some must-have greenhouse accessories:

- "Shelves and benches
- Doors and vents
- Ventilation and coolers
- Shade cloths
- Watering systems
- Heating
- Greenhouse grow-lights
- Ground and floor covering" (*What Must-Have Greenhouse Accessories Do I Really Need?* 2019).

What is a Cold Frame?

A cold frame is a plant shelter for your outdoor greenhouse. It is especially useful if you live somewhere colder. They protect your plants from the harsh winters. Think of it as a transparent insulator.

GROW A VEGETABLE GARDEN IN POTS AND CONTAINERS

It utilizes the sun's warmth to produce a safe microclimate for your greenhouse plants. You may find a smaller cold frame for your outdoor greenhouse. However, most cold frames are used for commercial gardening.

This was it for all the greenhouse basics. From indoors to outdoors, you know it all now.

Chapter Ten

Handling Herbs at Home

Not everything is about function. Any plant that is regarded as helpful is an herb. Some gardeners cultivate herbs purely for aesthetic reasons. The flavoring, medication, fragrance, dye, or other product may be derived from a plant's leaves, roots, seeds, stems, or flowers.

Why Herbs?

Growing herbs is hugely advantageous. They can elevate not only your cooking but also your garden!

Here are some benefits:

- "Working with fresh herbs is enjoyable; chiffonading, for example, has a really "chef-y" feel to it

- Fresh herbs enhance cuisine and truly bring out the flavor of your recipes

- The cost of purchasing herbs at the grocery store might vary

- You frequently wind up throwing away half the bundle of fresh herbs since most recipes only require a modest quantity

- Herb plants are stunning and have a wonderful aroma

- You do not require a patio or a lawn for cultivating herbs; they are quite simple to raise" (Wallace, n.d.)

Herb vs. Spice

People often make the mistake of using herbs and spices synonymously. The reality is that these two are entirely different from each other.

Herbs come from the fresher part of the plant, like the leaves. Spices, however, can come from the roots, stems, bark, fruits, or even seeds.

Herbs include thyme, oregano, basil, rosemary, parsley, etc. On the other hand, spices include cumin, cinnamon, ginger, coriander, anise, etc.

Grow Your Own Herbs!

Herbs are straightforward to grow. You can visit your local nursery and either buy seeds or young plants. Knowing whether the herb you want to raise is perennial or annual is important. Annual herbs include basil, coriander, and dill, while perennial ones are mint thyme and chives. We already know the difference between these two.

Annual herbs are best if the seeds are used to start their growth, while perennial herbs can be brought as seedlings and then planted in a warm spot.

Pots made up of ceramic, clay, wood, or plastic are fine as long as they have adequate drainage holes. Move them to a warm sunny spot whenever the weather allows it, and enjoy the results!

Herb Cuttings

Taking cuttings of your herb plants is an important step. It encourages the growth of the herb. You should do it in the spring or summer since the warm weather grows the plant. Lavender, mint, oregano, sage, and thyme are some excellent choices for cutting.

This is how you can start your cuttings:

- Select the tender segments (greener ones). It should be 5-6 inches long with about 5 leaves. Make a sharp, angled cut

- Remove the lower leaves and slip the end of the stem in rooting hormone powder. Plant 2 inches (5 centimeters) deep into some potting mix soil

- Cover loosely with a plastic bag for humidity

- Water when and if needed

Herbs Who Love the Shade

Even though most herbs love themselves some sun, some grow best in the shade. These shade-loving herbs require a minimum of 2 hours of sunlight per day. However, if you have less, it won't be much of a problem. You can still grow them. Plus, lack of sunlight might make them susceptible to the sun!

Following are some herbs that grow best in the shade:

Chervil | Cilantro | Coriander | Lemon Balm | Chive | Lemon Verbena | Dill | Parsley | Bay Leaf | Mint Tarragon

Here are some things that you need to keep in mind while growing these herbs:

- Avoid overfertilizing. It could make the plant weak

- Harvest regularly and keep cutting. It keeps the plant compact

- Look out for pests. Lack of sunlight makes them susceptible to the sun

- Horticultural or insecticide spray is important

INDOOR HERBS

The first step is to pick the right herb. If herbs can grow in shade or sunlight, they can surely grow indoors, right? This means opting for a plant that will thrive in indoor conditions. Some easy picks are basil, chives, mint, oregano, parsley, rosemary, and thyme.

You can either start with seeds or cuttings; your choice.

LIGHT

The key to growing indoor herbs is sunlight! A window or any other spot where the sunlight is maximum would be great. So, make sure to find a sunny location. They will be begging for it. You may even invest in some grow lights during the winters when the sunlight is less.

WATER

Herbs can sustain themselves in very little moisture. This clearly means that you shouldn't waterlog them by overwatering. So, take it easy on the water! The key is to keep the soil moist at all times for humidity.

THYME TO EAT

Herbs are a staple in cooking. Some kitchen staples include basil, parsley, bay leaf oregano, etc. All these are used in cooking, and each has an exquisite flavor. Italian and Mediterranean cuisine is incomplete without the addition of herbs.

- ***BASIL:*** has excellent flavor and is extremely popular in Mediterranean cuisines; fresh is better than dried. Example: pesto sauce and Caprese salad

- ***CILANTRO:*** strong smell, great with spicy foods, used as a garnish or cold preparations. Example: salsa, curries, and stir fry

- ***DILL:*** fresh is better than dried, coupled with good figs. Example: salads, dressings, meat dishes

- ***THYME:*** French cooking staple, intense flavor. Example: stews, soups, sauces, meat, and fish dishes

Note: when using dried herbs, try rubbing them between the palms or fingers. Increased surface area intensifies the flavor!

Medicinal Herbs

Herbs have been used for medicinal purposes for centuries. People of all cultures have been using them. Various herbs effectively treat common illnesses like colds, flu, cuts, inflammation, pain, digestive problems, anxiety, etc. (Foster, 1997).

These basic herbs can treat common issues:

ECHINACEA

- immunity booster
- fights viral and bacterial infections
- can be consumed as a tea by using dried flowers or root

CHAMOMILE

- natural sleep inducer
- relieves colic
- improves digestion
- encourages urination
- used for washing wounds
- helps inflammation
- consumed as tea from dried flowers

PERCY SARGEANT

YARROW

- first aid hero
- stanches blood flow
- relieves pain
- reduces inflammation
- apply crushed leaves to the wound or consume them as a tea

LEMON BALM

- reduces fevers and cold
- improves digestion
- calms anxiety
- controls the growth of bacteria and fungi
- consume as tea made up of fresh leaves

PEPPERMINT

- soothes stomach aches
- nervous stress
- colds
- fights bacteria and viruses
- consumed as a tea

GROW A VEGETABLE GARDEN IN POTS AND CONTAINERS

These are just a few herbs and their medicinal properties. Thousands of species exist and have been used for centuries to treat diseases and ailments.

This chapter focused on herbs, from everyday kitchen staples to medicinal ones. I hope the information and knowledge I have shared with you will be something that you can cherish and use as you start your gardening endeavor! I have included ways to grow them, care for them, etc.

Pass Forward Your Passion for Produce!

Now that you've got the gardening bug, you'll never look back... and you have the opportunity to ignite the passion in someone else.

Simply by leaving your honest opinion of this book on Amazon, you'll help other new gardeners find the guidance they need to set them on the road to success.

Thank you for your support. Fresh, homegrown produce should be accessible to everyone – and together, we can make sure that happens.

Conclusion

We have come so far, my gardening fellows!

I hope you all have learned a lot. I hope you have gleaned some helpful information about small-space gardening from this book. From delicious vegetables to medicinal herbs, there is hardly anything that I have left behind. So, whether you people want to garden for fun or want to be self-sufficient, this book will be with you throughout your fun journey.

Gardening is such a unique activity. Seeing the fruits of your efforts, and by that, I mean rewards, is a different kind of sentiment that you will only understand once you start harvesting. There are many gardening techniques, each with its own benefits. Do you have an empty backyard that you want to utilize? No problem, get your gardening gloves on!

Maybe you don't have enough space outside the house or apartment but really want to pursue your dream of having homegrown vegetables. Don't worry. Start indoor gardening! Get a greenhouse or just some pots; the options are endless.

PERCY SARGEANT

Self-sufficiency is quite liberating in itself. The best part of having your own garden is the fact that you will have organic produce at hand. Plus, nothing tastes as good as homegrown vegetables. Honestly. the aroma and freshness make it a class apart from those dusty grocery store ones.

Fresh herbs taste nothing like dried ones. They are easy to grow and a staple in every gardener's kitchen. In addition, herbs can elevate any and every dish you cook. Plus, if you start growing your own herbs, you're truly in a league of your own.

This book has been a testimonial to the experiences and knowledge I have gathered about plants over the years. From dormant seeds to full-blown fruits, it is truly a miraculous journey. The art of harvesting that particular vegetable is also something that you have to learn. Of course, time is key when gardening and growing your own vegetables and herbs.

By the end of this book, I am sure you will have many tips and tricks up your sleeve. I bet that this book has the power to turn a non-gardener into a gardener. I have busted many myths that people have about gardening. The idea that you can only garden if you have acres of space is really just false. You can garden wherever you want. Get a greenhouse if you like! I have given ample instructions about how to get one going, both indoors and outdoors.

Now that we have reached the end of this book, I hope you have realized that gardening is a great hobby and the key to being self-reliant. Being a plant parent is truly a rewarding job. You may consult this book throughout your gardening endeavor. As I've said before, the more you garden, the more you learn. Thus, I wish you all the luck! And since this book has helped you to start your journey, you might help it back by leaving an altruistic review!

Percy Sargeant Writer and Filmmaker

Percy Sargeant grew up in the countryside of England, where the 'country garden' wasn't just a figure of speech. The formal English garden consisted of wide paths bordered with deep yew hedges and glorious displays of flowers; roses, delphiniums, foxgloves, rhododendrons, lupins, statues, and structures with climbing honeysuckle, goldfish ponds, terraces, and lavishly planted pots. Traditional and timeless elements included lawns, an area for growing vegetables, a glass greenhouse, furniture, an orchard, and some topiary.

Percy and his family moved to the United States many years ago. He observed many English-style gardens all over the country, some more English than in England, in places like Chicago, Seattle, and Denver, displaying local botany species.

When he was a young lad, with his sister and their adventurous parents, they traveled to East Africa. They lived close to the Muhesi Game Reserve in Tanzania, their home becoming a menagerie of animal pets, which included a pair of Dalmatian dogs, a few ducks, a donkey, a beehive, and a local nocturnal primate with enormous eyes called a Galago, also known as a bush baby. Under these circumstances, as a child, Percy became fascinated by the natural world and the behavior of animals. His family moved back to the countryside of England, where they set up aviaries of exotic birds alongside dogs, cats, tortoises, and a variety of other creatures. And, of course, glorious plants, a greenhouse filled with the most exquisite orchids,

Percy had studied Botany and Zoology, the investigation of plants and animals. He was fascinated by the macro world of insects. As a child, he would collect insects to observe their behavior, and not once did he stab them through the abdomen to become mounted specimens. From this experience, he learned much about the need for patience, the inevitability of failure, and the preservation of life. He would go on to capture on film the behavior of insects and larger creatures, such as exotic birds, the grizzly bear, and many other species in between. His award-winning films were subsequently shown to countless audiences across the globe. Through these times, he became acutely aware of ecology and the need to preserve life and the environment.

His fascination with plants led to his involvement in nurturing garden crops and flowers in his California home and garden, growing tomatoes, beans, radishes, beets, and much more.

Percy, these days, based on his world experience, enjoys writing about plants to let others learn and experience the many rewards of growing plants of their own.

Percy has learned over the years to maintain a high level of respect for others, including the human species, and to maintain a good sense of humor a lot of the time!

Would you be so kind as to visit the Amazon review page and leave a review?

Acknowledgments

References

The 12 Principles of Plant Biology | American Society of Plant Biologists. (n.d.). American Society of Plant Biologists. Retrieved August 31, 2022, from https://aspb.org/education-outreach/k12-roots-and-shoots/the-12-principles-of-plant-biology-2/#toggle-id-1

Abercrombie, T. J. (2022, May 19). growing season | National Geographic Society. Resource Library. Retrieved August 31, 2022, from https://education.nationalgeographic.org/resource/growing-season

Albert, S. (n.d.). Grow Vegetables in the Right Season. Harvest to Table. Retrieved August 26, 2022, from https://harvesttotable.com/match_vegetable_crops_to_the/

Barton, R. (2022, April 6). Know Your Garden Soil: How to Make the Most of Your Soil Type. Eartheasy Guides & Articles. Retrieved August 22, 2022, from https://learn.eartheasy.com/articles/know-your-garden-soil-how-to-make-the-most-of-your-soil-type/

Bertelsen, K. (2020). Home » Vegetable Gardening How to Grow Vegetables & Flowers from Seed. the art of doing stuff. https://www.theartofdoingstuff.com/how-to-grow-vegetables-from-seed/#How_to_Plant_Vegetable_Seeds

Chadwick, P. (2020, October 5). Guidelines for Harvesting Vegetables. Piedmont Master Gardeners. Retrieved September 4, 2022, from https://piedmontmastergardeners.org/article/guidelines-for-harvesting-vegetables/

Composting: How to Make Compost using Tumblers & Bins. (n.d.). Eartheasy Guides & Articles. Retrieved August 23, 2022, from https://learn.eartheasy.com/guides/composting/

Dyer, M. H. (2022, January 10). How To Preserve Vegetables From Garden: Learn Methods Of Preserving Vegetables. Gardening Know How. Retrieved September 4, 2022, from https://www.gardeningknowhow.com/edible/vegetables/vgen/preserving-vegetables.htm

Edwards, W. M. (2022, July 19). All About Climate. National Geographic Society. Retrieved August 30, 2022, from https://education.nationalgeographic.org/resource/all-about-climate

Foster, S. (1997, March 1). Growing a Medicinal Herb Garden. Mother Earth Living. Retrieved September 6, 2022, from https://www.motherearthliving.com/gardening/Herbs-anyone-can-grow

Fountaine, S. (2016, August 15). How to Preserve Veggies in Olive Oil! Feasting At Home. Retrieved September 4, 2022, from https://www.feastingathome.com/olive-oil-preserved-vegetables/

Gill, D. (2017, November 10). Plant fall and winter vegetables. LSU AgCenter. Retrieved August 26, 2022, from https://lsuagcenter.com/profiles/rbogren/articles/page1510330147968

Grant, A. (2021, June 24). Desert Vegetables And Flowers - Growing Non-Drought Tolerant Desert Plants. Gardening Know-How. Retrieved August 22, 2022, from https://www.gardeningknowhow.com/edible/vegetables/vgen/vegetables-in-the-desert.htm

Grant, A. (2022, April 12). Storing Veggies In Sand - Learn About Sand Storing Root Vegetables. Gardening Know-How. Retrieved September 4, 2022, from https://www.gardeningknowhow.com/edible/vegetables/vgen/storing-root-crops-in-sand.htm

Guide, S., & Gemeš, N. (2021, November 10). Everything You Need To Know About An Indoor Greenhouse. GreenCitizen. Retrieved September 5, 2022, from https://greencitizen.com/blog/indoor-greenhouse/#t-1595170314232

Huffstetler, E. (2022, May 19). 55 Perennial Vegetables, Fruits, Herbs and Nuts. The Spruce. Retrieved August 26, 2022, from https://www.thespruce.com/perennial-foods-1388677

Iannotti, M. (2021, November 8). Identifying Plant Pests and Diseases. The Spruce. Retrieved August 29, 2022, from https://www.thespruce.com/insects-and-diseases-of-plants-4070266

Lee, H. (2020, June 26). 10 Natural Alternatives to Chemical Preservatives – Mosaic. Mosaic Foods. Retrieved September 4, 2022, from https://www.mosaicfoods.com/blogs/main/10-natural-alternatives-to-chemical-preservatives

Miller, L. (2021, June 3). Harvesting For Beginners: Garden Harvesting For First Time Gardeners. Gardening Know-How. Retrieved September 3, 2022, from https://www.gardeningknowhow.com/edible/vegetables/vgen/harvesting-for-beginners.htm

Murphy, E. (n.d.). Summer Vegetables - Which Veggies Grow the Best in Summer? Gilmour. Retrieved August 26, 2022, from https://gilmour.com/summer-vegetable-garden

National Organic Program | Agricultural Marketing Service. (n.d.). Agricultural Marketing Service. Retrieved August 23, 2022, from https://www.ams.usda.gov/about-ams/programs-offices/national-organic-program

Catherine. (2020, December 21). 60 inspirational gardening quotes and garden sayings. Growing Family. https://growingfamily.co.uk/garden-tips/60-inspirational-gardening-quotes-garden-sayings

Printed in Great Britain
by Amazon